PRAISE FOR *EMPOWI*

"Splendidly written from a teacher's perspective with practical examples explaining personalized learning and how to offer choice to all learners. My intellectual gears have been reenergized by thinking about intrinsic opportunities for students to reach their full potential. This is a must-read for educators seeking inspiration and ideas for learner empowerment!"

—**Kristen Slechta,** professional learning specialist

"Understanding personalized learning is one thing; putting it into action is another. Andrew has found a way to do both. I love that this book is laid out in such a practical manner. As someone who has followed Andrew's work for a while and collaborated with him on many occasions, I can assure you he gets it and has written an amazing book that will help you get it, too!"

—**Andi McNair,** innovation/gifted education specialist and author

"*Empowered to Choose* is a must-read for educators looking to reclaim the art of teaching in today's all too often scripted profession. Andrew masterfully embeds theory, research, and personal experience into an easy-to-use resource. Starting from the nuances between individualization, differentiation, and personalization, he builds a foundational understanding and introduces his audience to strategies they can easily implement. Educators will find themselves continually revisiting *Empowered to Choose* for ideas as the needs of their students change."

—**Dr. Stephanie Dredge,** senior director of specialized services and supports

"*Empowered to Choose* by Andrew Easton is an essential book for educators looking to improve their teaching practice by providing meaningful, choice-infused personalized learning for students. Andrew starts with the most important question—'Why?'—and shares how personalized learning benefits students. He provides educators with the resources, framework, and inspiration they need to reflect on our practice so that we can truly provide the best learning experiences for all students. The book is full of examples, strategies, and authentic stories that will provide readers with inspiration, motivation, and actionable steps to create personalized learning in their classrooms. *Empowered to Choose* provides everything that educators need to feel confident in implementing the most meaningful and personalized learning experiences for all students. It is a must-read for every educator wanting to empower students."

—Rachelle Dené Poth, educator, author, consultant, attorney

EMPOWERED TO CHOOSE

ANDREW EASTON

EMPOWERED TO CHOOSE

A PRACTICAL GUIDE TO PERSONALIZED LEARNING

Published by Dave Burgess Consulting, Inc.
San Diego, CA
DaveBurgessConsulting.com

Library of Congress Control Number: 2022946547
Paperback ISBN: 978-1-956306-37-8
Ebook ISBN: 978-1-956306-38-5

Cover and interior design by Liz Schreiter
Edited and produced by Reading List Editorial
ReadingListEditorial.com

To my father and grandfather. Though neither of you had the chance to read this, your influence is on every page. In that way, this book is dedicated to all educators who know that they will never grasp the full impact of their efforts and lead anyway, confident that their good work will long outlive them.

CONTENTS

Preface 1

Introduction: What Is Personalized Learning? 5

Chapter 1: The *Why* Behind Personalizing Learning 11

Chapter 2: Rethinking Our Approach to Personalizing
           Learning 20

Chapter 3: How to Personalize Learning 27

Chapter 4: Four Strategies That Support Personalized
           Practices 37

Chapter 5: Learner Choice in Topic 43

Chapter 6: Learner Choice in Instructional Delivery 54

Chapter 7: Learner Choice in Learning Strategy 62

Chapter 8: Learner Choice in Product (Assessment) 70

Chapter 9: Learner Choice in Pace 82

Chapter 10: Learner Choice in Communication 91

Chapter 11: Learner Choice in Learning Space 97

Chapter 12: Layering Multiple Learner-Choice Opportunities
            into the Learning 104

Chapter 13: Brainstorming for Entry Points 108

Chapter 14: Measuring the Impact of This Work 111

Chapter 15: Conclusion 115

Acknowledgments 117

About Andrew Easton 118

Bibliography 119

More from Dave Burgess Consulting, Inc. 121

PREFACE

Teaching is, without question, among the most noble of professions. People don't go into education for the money or for accolades; they choose to become teachers because they have big hearts for helping others and want to do work that is meaningful. They choose to teach because they want to spend their days creating experiences for kids that will have a positive and lasting influence on them. For many of us, we believe in that purpose because we felt it when we ourselves were in school. Most educators can point to a teacher whose role in their own life was so profound that they chose to become a teacher themselves, because they wanted to make that kind of difference in the life of someone else. For me, that teacher was my dad.

I'm the fourth Andrew Easton in my family. My father and grandfather before me were both teacher-coaches. It's kind of the family business. My Grandpa Easton taught industrial tech and had a long tenure as a head football coach at the high school level. His teams won an impressive 163 games during his career, a feat due in no small part to his amazing assistant coach, my dad. My father was a business teacher and coached with my grandpa for most of my adolescence, and so I spent a fair amount of my childhood at practice and on the sidelines watching the two of them teach and lead.

Their goal was always to help their student-athletes to become not just better players but better people. I heard that message consistently preached at every practice and in every pre- and postgame speech. It shaped every teachable moment that the two of them unfailingly seized. Their message was consistent. It was clear. Use this game as a way to develop an approach to how you will live your life hereafter. Learn to live with purpose, with intentionality, and with passion.

I loved those days. I miss those days.

Living in a small town, we would frequently run into their former students. When we did, it would always make me smile when someone, who by most measures was a complete stranger to me, would tell me just how influential my grandpa and dad had been in shaping the person they had become. I was always so deeply proud of them. I am still incredibly proud of them to this day, even though they are no longer with us.

There is one instance that sticks out from when I was around ten years old. My dad and I were walking to our car, having just wrapped up another after-school practice. As we walked, he asked me if I knew what the difference was between a good teacher or coach and a great one. I obviously had no idea. I had never even considered it. He sensed my hesitation and said, "A good coach will create a successful system and ask the players to fit into the program, but that can only get you so far. A great coach will design a system that brings out the best in each individual on the team. And the same thing is true for the classroom."

It's been almost thirty years since my dad gave me that advice, and having spent over fifteen years in this profession, having had countless opportunities to collaborate with educators from all over the world, I must admit that his point still holds up. Great leaders establish relationships that make others feel recognized and understood, and then they use that bond and knowledge to design an experience that will truly test the individual in such a way that pushes them a little closer toward their full potential. That's coaching. That's teaching at its best. It's an incredibly inspiring thing to witness when you see someone who has learned how to support and motivate others to become more than they themselves ever thought possible. I have always believed that our profession holds the power to have that kind of an impact on kids, because I saw it first in my dad.

From the time I was a kid, I've known that the work of an educator is personal. I've known that our aim is always higher than any test score or *W* in a win-loss column. We work with children and young adults, and the goal is to play a part in helping them take the next meaningful step forward. How we do that is unique to each of us. That's what makes teaching an art. We work hard, we play to our strengths, and over time, we develop a tool kit of activities, strategies, and routines that help us be effective practitioners of learning. We get good at supporting kids.

But it's like my dad said, most of us develop systems that work for us, and we invite our students to join in and fulfill their role as a part of our program. And to be fair, doing that makes a lot of sense. We care about kids, and we appreciate routines (so do our students), and so we design systems and utilize strategies that fit the rhythms of how we like to operate in our day-to-day lives. It's something we can run. It's something we can control. It's something that, by most traditional measures, works really well toward ensuring there's a high floor for student achievement. And while I know the old saying "If it ain't broke, don't fix it," I know too that Stephen Covey warned that good is the enemy of great.[1]

Now, you might be asking yourself, What could be better than a school system full of highly effective teachers? And my answer is a school system full of highly effective learners.

So let's start there. The conversation in this book is focused on that aim. The pursuit of great is the pursuit of learner-centered *and*

---

1 Jim Collins, *Good to Great: Why Some Companies Make the Leap ... and Others Don't* (New York: Collins, 2009).

learner-driven learning experiences. These two are not the same thing. Having the opportunity to lead does not mean you have the ability to do so (yet), and where that ability is lacking, we need to step into those spaces and develop it with and within our learners. We need to coach them up. However, to do so will ask you to shift what you're striving for as their teacher, because student success has a lot less to do with what you can do for your students and a lot more to do with what they can do for themselves.

WHAT IS PERSONALIZED LEARNING?

I f you were to ask a room of educators to explain what personalized learning is, you would likely get a fairly consistent answer. You would hear things like, "It's learners going at their own pace," "It's learning that is in some way tailored to the individual student," and "There's often an element of choice to it."

But if you were to ask that same group what personalized learning looks like in practice, there would likely be a much broader range of responses. Some educators associate choice boards with personalization. Others see it in genius hour, passion projects, and project-based learning (PBL). Tech-savvy teachers might turn to programs or apps that differentiate the types of challenges, materials, and assessments students receive, while there are also those who contend that collaborative conversations about identifying learning goals or designing learning pathways is the key.

There are also entire school systems that have made the self-paced piece their top priority, and as a result have rearranged everything from curriculum calendars to the school-day schedule itself. In some districts, this has even brought about an end to what we recognize as the traditional grade-level progression and grading systems. But here's the thing—you can change the tech, you can change the pacing guide, and you can change an A to whatever you want to call it, a 4 or an M, but if you don't change the practices to focus on equipping learners with the skills and strategies necessary to be successful as learners, instead of striving to simply be great at the game of school, you'll end up creating more problems than you solve.

While the pursuit of each of these practices is admirable and in most cases a marked improvement from the traditional one-size-fits-all approach to education, you might be surprised to learn that most of them are not examples of personalization. Eliminating this ambiguity around what is or isn't personalized is essential to moving this work forward because historically, that lack of specificity has left educators confused or disillusioned by personalized learning.

So from the start, know that this book is committed to reclaiming the term *personalized learning* and to providing an explicit and practical approach for how to implement these practices into any classroom setting. For this to happen, you will need to maintain a growth mindset. Expect to learn a great deal about personalizing learning. Expect to relearn and feel affirmed in some of the work you are already doing. Finally, expect that there will likely be the need to unlearn some assumptions you currently carry about how this work should look.

So what does it look like to personalize learning?

To arrive at that deeper level of clarity of action, we first need greater clarity of purpose. By the end of this introduction, you will learn the definition of *personalized learning* and have a clear understanding of what personalization is versus what it is not. You can then bring that knowledge to chapter one and see how it aligns with the *why* behind this work. Chapters two and three will first frame how to think about designing personalized learning practices and then delve into a practical approach to guide your planning process. Then the rest of the book is dedicated to a framework within which you can explore classroom-tested examples and implementation advice that comes from experience with this work. In short, this book is dedicated to helping educators develop a practical approach to personalizing learning in their grade level, content area, and context.

DEFINING PERSONALIZED LEARNING

The chief aim of personalization has always been to foster greater student agency in the learners we serve. The Aurora Institute, an organization at the forefront of the conversations around personalization, shared the following in a 2017 blog post titled "Policies for Personalization: Student Agency":

> Personalization and student agency go hand in hand—it is nearly impossible for teachers to manage a personalized classroom if students are constantly turning to them for direction. Thus, as schools move toward personalized . . . education, they will also want to create the conditions for students to take ownership over their education (i.e., student agency).[1]

If the edu-jargon of *student agency* is a tough term to wrap your mind around, here's a simple way to think about it. I once recorded a podcast with Kathleen McClaskey, coauthor of *How to Personalize Learning*, and during our conversation, she shared that, to her, student agency refers to a learner's ability to act. I've also heard others associate student agency with any situation where learners can assume responsibility over their learning and take an active role in that process instead of having school "done *to* them." It's learner centered and also learner driven, and those two things are not the same.

Holding those ideals in mind, we can continue to build clarity around what it means to personalize learning by acknowledging what personalization is not. This is important because too often we call

---

1 Chris Sturgis, "Policies for Personalization: Student Agency," Aurora Institute (blog), November 1, 2016, aurora-institute.org/cw_post/policies-for-personalization-student-agency/.

differentiated or individualized practices personalization because of the aspects that each has in common with personalized learning.

First, let's look at differentiation. According to Sarah D. Sparks, assistant editor, reporter, and data journalist for *Education Week*, differentiated instruction is "the process of identifying students' individual learning strengths, needs, and interests and adapting lessons to match them."[2] This definition is similar to Dr. Jim Rickabaugh's definition of personalization in his book *Tapping the Power of Personalized Learning*, where Rickabaugh wrote that personalization is "an approach to learning and instruction that is designed around individual learner readiness, strengths, needs, and interests."[3] The two sound almost identical, right? Both differentiation and personalization strive to tailor the learning to better meet the strengths, needs, and interests of the individual learner, but who each designates as being responsible for designing that experience is notably different.

Differentiation traditionally looks like the teacher developing multiple tiers of instruction, materials, and assessments so that students can be tracked into a pathway that is more aligned with their ability level than the whole-class, single-lesson approach provides. Personally, I can appreciate differentiated instruction, but it's not an example of personalized learning for two reasons. First, the teacher is still the one doing all the work of designing the experience. The students, having gone through the differentiated learning, are no better prepared to design and drive their own process than when they started. The second reason is that tracking by ability tailors the learning to each ability group, not the individual, and the aspiration of personalization is to have the learning tailored to, and ultimately by, each student.

Similarly, it's important to note that individualized learning is not personalization. In a 2018 article for ISTE, Dale Basye defined

---

2 Sarah D. Sparks, "Differentiated Instruction: A Primer," Education Week, January 28, 2015, edweek.org/teaching-learning/differentiated-instruction-a-primer/2015/01.

3 James Rickabaugh, *Tapping the Power of Personalized Learning: A Roadmap for School Leaders* (Alexandria, VA: ASCD, 2016).

individualized instruction as "instruction calibrated to meet the unique pace of various students."[4] While adjusting the pace of learning is a goal that both individualization and personalization share, it's once again important to consider who is responsible for calibrating learning to meet the individual's unique pace. Speaking as a teacher myself, I once had 151 students across the six sections I taught. Maybe it's just me, but it seems literally impossible for a teacher to be responsible for tailoring the pace of the learning for each of those 151 individuals.

A more practical approach to individualization has been to rely on technology and artificial intelligence to do this work. Today, there are a number of programs that administer assessments and use that data to curate the topics or concepts the learners need to revisit or move onto according to their scores. This method for individualizing the learning experience is impressive and valuable; I honestly hope to see more of this work as technology continues to advance. But if fostering student agency is important, then leaning on an AI-driven program to tailor the pace of the learning teaches learners very little to nothing about how to independently manage learning on their own.

This leads us to some basic characteristics of personalization that we can use as criteria for evaluating if an experience is personalized or not. Here's what we know to be true about personalized learning:

1. Learners need to be at the center of the learning process.
2. Learners need to be the designers and drivers of the learning process.
3. Learners need to design and drive their learning with academic intentionality in a way that optimizes their experience, retention, mastery, or all three.

If we meld these goals with Dr. Rickabaugh's definition of personalization, the process of personalizing learning starts to become clear.

---

4   Dale Basye, "Personalized vs. Differentiated vs. Individualized Learning," ISTE (blog), January 24, 2018, iste.org/explore/Education-leadership/Personalized-vs.-differentiated-vs.-individualized -learning.

The definition for personalized learning that we will build our practices upon is the following:

LEARNING IS PERSONALIZED WHEN LEARNERS HAVE BOTH THE OPPORTUNITY AND THE ABILITY TO STRATEGICALLY TAILOR THE EXPERIENCE TO OPTIMALLY SUIT THEIR INDIVIDUAL LEARNING STRENGTHS, PREFERENCES, INTERESTS, AND/OR NEEDS.

For our conversations about personalization, this definition will not be some abstract placeholder of a theoretical idea. It's instead a road map, and the pieces of this definition will directly influence how we think about and practically approach the personalization of learning.

CHAPTER 1

THE *WHY* BEHIND PERSONALIZING LEARNING

Designing learning experiences that are personalized by the learner is work that I am incredibly passionate about and have been invested in since the end of my first year of teaching over fifteen years ago. Back then, my teaching assignment included four sections of senior English, and I can still remember watching my first group of students graduate. One by one, they took the stage to receive their diplomas, and as I sat there watching, I was hit with an overwhelming sense of guilt that I had somehow let them down. Why? Well, because in that moment, I knew that most of them were underprepared to handle the workload and responsibilities of college or a career, and that fact filled me with anxiety and concern.

This led me to ask myself a hard question: What is it, specifically, that they need to improve upon? The simple answer was soft skills. It was all the little things—things like the ability to stay organized, to manage time effectively, to communicate professionally and constructively with others, and to advocate for themselves—that we as adults know become big things that are essential for personal and professional confidence and success.

Curious to learn more, I spent time that summer researching online to see if anyone else was asking the same questions as I was about soft skills. Eventually, I came across a finance article that shared a list of the top ten traits that employers were looking for in their new hires. Imagine the slow and steady rise of my angst as I read each individual trait and realized that these ten were the very things I saw as deficiencies in my students. Clearly something had to change.

My initial effort came in the first week of school that fall, when I shared that top-ten list of desirable new-hire traits with my students. In every section, we talked about each trait, and then I made the class a promise. If there came a time when what we were doing did not in some way address one of those traits, they were to call me out on it, and we would quit doing whatever it was we were doing. That promise forced me to lesson plan with a secondary goal of fostering soft skills. Adding that lens was the start of what I would later recognize as an integral part of the planning process for personalization.

On Fridays, I would survey my students, asking them to evaluate the degree to which they felt they had an opportunity to develop each trait during the learning that week. It wasn't long before a problem emerged from their feedback: one trait was receiving the lowest score every time students took the survey.

This all came to a head in October, when one student brought her survey to me and said, "Mr. Easton, I don't know why you even keep putting *Flexibility* on these surveys. I mean, this is school. There's nothing flexible about it. Teachers tell us what to do and we're supposed to do what they say. There's no flexibility in that!"

I don't know if it was the tone of her blunt remark or what I recognized immediately as the truth behind it that was more cutting. Her point was valid, and to be honest, it made me angry. I didn't see myself as a dictator, and I didn't appreciate hearing that this was her perception of my profession. But her comment did make me want to do something about it. So once I calmed down, my first thought was, I wonder what it would look like if students had the flexibility to control the pace of an entire unit . . . and that's exactly what we did three months later.

In January of that school year, I launched a seven-week unit where students could advance through the materials at their own pace for the duration of that time frame. I'll admit that I knew very little about how to support learners in that setting, but they appreciated the chance to be in charge for a change and gave me grace and their questions to help guide us through the growing pains of that first iteration.

What was startling to watch was the differences in each learner's approach to their work. For example, some took all their reading home because they felt that they couldn't get lost in a book at school, while others read almost exclusively at school, citing that their home environment wasn't conducive for sustained, silent reading. Some students worked better in groups with partners who could keep them accountable, while others found that they could better focus when working alone on independent tasks. Our special education supports became more fluid, with identified learners moving in and out of the services as needed. And when several students in each section finished all seven weeks' worth of coursework in half the time, I knew this was an approach to teaching and learning that had to continue.

It wasn't all roses. It should come as no surprise that the majority of the learners struggled to stay organized, productive, and motivated across the seven-week span of time. But that was the whole point, right? The learners needed to experience this productive struggle; without it, I'm not sure how else they would have grown in the same ways. It was hard for them, but it was also healthy, and when graduation came around that May, I felt a sense of peace with the progress those students had made.

Over the next ten years of teaching, roughly half of every course I taught was conducted in a similar format. Students would be given all the assignments, resources, and expectations up front, along with a deadline by which all or some of that work was due. Iteration became the mother of invention as my professional growth routinely came from observing, engaging, and listening to learners as they navigated being at the center of the experience. Each new piece of feedback refined my approach to supporting their efforts, and eventually, I learned enough to turn my reactive realizations into proactive practices. I started front-loading a variety of learning strategies that students could pick from and use. (We will explore many of those strategies later in this book.) What I came to realize was this: teaching learners *how* to learn is much more impactful than teaching them *what* to learn. That belief is at the heart of personalized learning.

Now, I've always believed that luck comes to those who are too busy working to look for it, but I know too that it takes some luck for any good endeavor to get off the ground. Thankfully, that's what happened next. I got really lucky. As I started sharing this work with others, I was fortunate that educators began to invite me in to present and co-design personalized learning experiences with teachers at all levels across the United States. While not every design has been built around pace, the consistent theme in this work has been thinking through ways to teach learners how to tailor the learning experience for themselves. It's been exhilarating to grow these practices with other educators and watch it have a profound impact on all students, seniors to kindergarteners, across all content areas.

I've also been quite lucky to have had a chance to get to know many of the thought leaders in the area of personalizing learning on a personal level. Those rich conversations with leaders in this field have grounded my understanding of the *why* behind this work. That list would include educators like Dr. Jim Rickabaugh, author of *Tapping the Power of Personalized Learning*; Allison Zmuda, coauthor of *Students at the Center*; and Kathleen McClaskey, coauthor of *How to Personalize Learning*. These leaders are all phenomenal, and I would point you to their respective texts, as those books create a robust case for the need for personalized learning.

Instead of taking a deep dive into an end of the pool that is already full with justifications for the *why* behind this work, let's keep it simple and focus on three specific *why*s about personalization that validate the learner's need to experience learning that is personalized. This will afford us more time to explore the *how* and some classroom-tested examples in the later chapters.

THREE WHYS ABOUT PERSONALIZED LEARNING

Why PL #1: Personalized Learning Prepares Students to Be Effective Lifelong Learners in a Digital Age

What is the point of education today, if not to equip our youth with the skills necessary to be effective, tech-savvy learners in a digital age? A digital age when learners have devices that can answer nearly every knowledge-level question they could possibly conceive. A digital age when learners have access to an infinite number of resources, blogs, sites, threads, podcasts, and video clips that can help educate them on any endeavor they could ever possibly seek to undertake. A digital age when learners are leveraging augmented and virtual realities and artificial intelligences to engage in immersive experiences and simulations that were previously the stuff of science fiction. The Gen Z learner has more tools for creativity at their disposal than the human race has ever had available at one time, along with 24-7 access to an infinite number of avenues through which to collaborate and share with others.

Having acknowledged that, there is an unspoken temptation to think of this as being some futuristic reality that our students will age into at some point, and that's just not the case. It's here. It's now. And by the way, we educators are immersed in it, too, whether we have embraced the technology that is at our disposal or not. Accepting this as our present reality means accepting that the twenty-first-century teacher is no longer the lone conduit of information, and truthfully, we need to teach like it. If that thought bothers you, let me offer some encouragement: Technology doesn't diminish our role, it expands it.

Those invested in blended learning know that to be true. For years, educators have been blending technology with time-tested best practices to enhance learning. More recently, that work has grown and innovation has occurred when teachers have used the tech creatively as a catalyst for real pedagogical change. Think of the higher end of the SAMR model. These changes brought new potential to the profession; they raised the ceiling for what's possible, instructionally. And these efforts were only amplified by the uncomfortable shifts that took place during the various learning scenarios of the COVID-19 pandemic.

Personalization is the next step forward in the integration of technology into the learning process, but we can't make that dream a reality without first dramatically shifting how we think about our work. Teachers care so much for the kiddos they serve that they often feel that it is their duty to make sure that every student learns. To personalize learning, we have to recognize that we are *not* responsible for the learning, but we are responsible for the people responsible for the learning. In practice, this means that we don't simply design learning experiences for our students; we design experiences that teach learners how *they* might design the learning experiences for themselves, and technology plays a vital role in that.

Tech affords learners more avenues for learning, collaborating, and creating, and personalization is poised to seize the potential of these diverse options by empowering learners to choose the tools and strategies that work best for them at each and every step of the learning process. Without those options, there would be no choice, and without choice, we would be back to the monolith—the single-track, whole-class lesson plan.

When used this way, tech integration evolves past blended and into personalized learning as the tools and resources are now being selected and optimally utilized by the students instead of their teachers. The value added here is that by actively making decisions about their learning pathways, the learners are forced into a metacognitive space that is a significant departure from the familiar "playing the game of school." It's a simulation of the autonomy we all experience when it is up to us to learn on our own, and like anything else, practice leads to preparedness, in the present and the future.

Why PL #2: Personalized Learning Supports Growth in All Learners Across the Achievement Gap

In first and second grade my daughter, Amour, really struggled with learning how to read. As her dad (and an English teacher), it broke my heart to watch her give her best effort and still end up in tears, throwing books across the room in frustration. That said, I am forever grateful to the reading specialist at my daughter's school who started meeting with her regularly to offer one-on-one support. That intervention led to a dramatic change in her ability to read, and by the end of third grade, she was staying up late at night to read chapter books.

What did this reading specialist do to transform my daughter as a reader? Well, initially, she shifted Amour's mindset about reading, explaining to her that she simply had not yet found the right strategies that could help her improve. Then they systematically experimented with a variety of reading strategies, and when they found the right ones for Amour, things clicked. Her approach to reading and her fluency rate have never been the same since.

I share this story because in every classroom there is an achievement gap, and it's incredibly difficult to address those gaps because the needs of each individual are so diverse and nuanced. Historically, teachers have turned to differentiation to address this issue, but how is it that a learner is supposed to grow when they are being tracked into coursework where the bar for content and assignments has been lowered? My daughter didn't need easier books to learn how to read; she needed a new approach to reading, and that's the kind of thinking that personalization promotes.

Teaching students how to become better learners holds a similar benefit for our students in the middle and also our high-ability learners as well. When working with HAL students, teachers routinely share that they feel the "need to do more to challenge them," and the common practice for how to do this (which is always well intended) is to give them additional work when they finish early. Interestingly enough, it has been my experience that many high-ability learners are among the weakest students in terms of their approach to learning because things have always come so easily to them that they don't develop a process for how to work through things when they struggle. Personalization pushes our HAL students to grow as learners, just as it does their peers across the ability spectrum.

Why PL #3: Personalized Learning Prepares Learners for a Future Where Hybrid and Remote Work-from-Home Scenarios Are Increasingly Prevalent

For years, we have acknowledged that the US educational system has been stuck in a mode that is better suited to the industrialization age, for which it was initially created, than the demands of the moment. While education reform has been consistently slow, technological advancements have only accelerated the evolution of the way we work, leaving schools perpetually two steps behind the times, trying to catch up.

In 2020, the COVID-19 pandemic hit, and for many people the workplace shifted from the office to their home. During that time, employers and their employees experienced the pros and cons of a more flexible work environment and schedule, and what some perceived as the future of work suddenly became the present reality.

There are those who would question how prevalent and sustainable a hybrid or remote work environment is for the workforce moving forward. However, a 2021 Upwork report projects that "36.2 million workers or 22 percent of Americans will be working remotely by the year 2025," which would be an 87 percent increase from prepandemic levels.[1] Additionally, Microsoft CEO Satya Nadella was quoted in a 2021 article titled "The Next Great Disruption Is Hybrid Work—Are We Ready?" as saying, "Over the past year, no area has undergone more rapid transformation than the way we work. Employee expectations are changing, and we will need to define productivity much more broadly—inclusive of collaboration, learning, and wellbeing to drive career advancement for every worker, including frontline and knowledge workers, as well as for new graduates and those who are in the workforce today. All this needs to be done with flexibility in when, where, and how people work."[2]

What then should be the response of those in education to this transformational shift in the way we work?

If the US educational system does not find an answer to this question, it is in danger of falling dramatically behind the demands of the work world that it is committed to preparing learners to enter. There is a need for an equally dramatic shift in best practices in the ways Nadella points out. If schools are to prepare learners for a future where work is "done with flexibility in when, where, and how people work," then learners need, at the very least, more opportunities to develop skills like the ability to self-regulate their efforts and enhance their productivity when working independently.

Personalized learning experiences equip learners with the soft skills and sense of agency necessary for them to thrive in an in-person or remote work setting.

---

1 Adam Ozimek, "Future Workforce Report 2021: How Remote Work Is Changing Business Forever," Upwork, September 28, 2021, upwork.com/research/future-workforce-report.

2 Satya Nadella, quoted in "The Next Great Disruption Is Hybrid Work—Are We Ready?," Microsoft, March 22, 2021, microsoft.com/en-us/worklab/work-trend-index/hybrid-work.

CHAPTER 2

RETHINKING OUR APPROACH TO PERSONALIZING LEARNING

As our conversation shifts from the *why*s behind personalization to the *how*, we must hold to those *why*s and bend how we approach personalization to meet those outcomes. In saying that, I'm reminded of the words of Pete Hall, coauthor of *Creating a Culture of Reflective Practice*, who wrote in that text that "shifting action does not always result in shifted thinking, but shifting thinking *always* results in shifted action."[1] In the spirit of Hall's words, let's be clear from the start that this chapter is a thought exercise for how to think about designing personalized learning *experiences*. This shift in perspective will be foundational to the more explicit instruction in the chapter that follows, where we will explore how to utilize choice to achieve the aim of personalization.

To begin with, it's important to point out that Hall's statement fails to mention that shifting thinking is no simple task. It's often the case that the heaviest lifting done with any new initiative is not in the demands of carrying out the work, but instead in the unlearning and rethinking required to reimagine the approach.

This is true of personalization in education.

---

1   Pete Hall and Alisa A. Simeral, *Creating a Culture of Reflective Practice: Capacity Building for Schoolwide Success* (Alexandria, VA: ASCD, 2017).

For nearly sixteen years now, there has been a great deal of work done under the moniker of *personalized learning*, which means most educators reading this will have some preconceived notions about what a "fully personalized" experience is supposed to look like. Before reading on, I would ask you to pause and reflect on that. What are your prior perceptions? And then quietly set them aside for the moment.

Why? Well, because to hold on to them would be a backward way of designing a model worth following. Again, *how* we approach our work should be driven by our *why*, not someone else's *what*. I caution against this because I know this is happening. I hear it very clearly every time teachers share about the work they are doing and feel the need to open with, "Well, it's not 'fully personalized,' but . . . " Whether it's out of humility or self-doubt, we cannot apologetically downplay our efforts as we try to carry out what we know is in the best interest of our students. Give yourself some grace and some credit, and be careful not to let some contrived ideal sit in a place of judgment over what you do on behalf of the kids you serve.

Speaking of that ideal, here's the big question we need to consider when rethinking our approach to personalizing learning: Is the goal of personalization for the teacher to design a fully personalized learning experience, or for the learners to develop the ability to navigate and tailor the learning according to their own purposes? If the latter is true, then that shifts what we do in the classroom in the pursuit of that outcome.

To give this question some clarity, let's look at this idea in another context.

I am the head coach of my son's first-grade basketball team. Now that's a perspective shifter, let me tell you! It's been fun. The kids are great, and they've learned a lot, but we had to start small. They knew what it meant to pass, shoot, and dribble, but terms like *rebound* and phrases like *set a screen* meant nothing to them. They needed time to learn, and I'm happy to say that we have made substantial progress this season, but I'm not quite ready yet to judge our squad compared to the '96 Bulls! The '96 Bulls might be the closest thing to the basketball ideal that there has ever been, but frankly, that's just not where our first graders are at this point in their basketball journey, and I don't have to apologize for that. Instead, I try to focus on breaking the game down into its component parts and doing the meaningful work of skill development across each of the various aspects of the game: dribbling, passing, shooting, rebounding, screening, and others. We practice to learn, and over time, we've learned enough to play.

Maybe it's the coach in me, but I approach personalizing learning the same way. Sure, whatever comes to mind when you think of a fully personalized experience sounds great, but I'm more inclined to break it down into its component parts and consider what it might look like for learners to get better at each individual aspect of the whole process of learning. If that's where the students are, then that's where we need to meet them with this work.

The first step then is to break down the definition for personalized learning we constructed in the introduction into its component parts. From there we can begin to think about how we might achieve this process in practice.

Learning is personalized when learners have both the opportunity and the ability to strategically tailor the experience to optimally suit their individual learning strengths, preferences, interests, and/or needs.

This definition has three components that are important to tease out. Those components are *the opportunity*, *the ability*, and what we will collectively refer to as *the drivers* (the individual's learning strengths, preferences, interests, and/or needs). These three components must work in harmony with one another for personalization to occur. This chapter will explain all three components in detail and point out where each typically breaks down. When an educator is able to design, teach, and lead in such a way that fosters a classroom culture where these three components are understood and owned by each learner, the students stand to experience the greatest gains possible in terms of their growth in student agency and soft-skill development.

THE OPPORTUNITY

During the fall of 2020, I was fortunate to take part in a video-conferencing call with John Hattie, education researcher and author of *Visible Learning*. Hattie is known for his meta-analysis of quantitative measures of the effect size of different factors on educational outcomes. In short, his research assigned a number value and a hierarchy for over 250 factors that influence learning. Near the end of our time with John, a colleague of mine asked him what is the number-one piece of advice he would impart to teachers to improve their instruction. Without hesitation, Hattie responded, "Well, it might be a bit crude to say, but 'Just shut up.'" To be fair, Hattie said this in jest and certainly for effect, but his point was clear: teachers need to spend less time talking *at* students and more time affording them the opportunity to lead their own learning.

In the introduction, we highlighted that learners need to be at the center of the learning experience. That's the *opportunity* being referenced here. Thankfully, few teachers need to be convinced of the value of learner-centered learning. Most acknowledge that active participation and student ownership over the learning process is desirable. However, believing in these ideals does not always translate into transformed practices, and there are several reasons for that.

One reason is that many educators have not experienced learner-centered learning in their own formative education. With little to no personal experience in this format, it can be challenging for teachers to wrap their minds around what it might look like to teach that way in their classrooms. To them, it's not a conscious choice to avoid putting the learner at the center, they simply can't envision it.

Another reason that often goes unspoken among educators is that leading whole-class learning can be more comfortable for the teacher because it's fairly predictable and easy to facilitate. Think about it—with the right routines in place and a decent grasp on classroom management, a teacher who follows the pattern of leading whole-group instruction, transitioning into independent work time, and finishing the session with a closure activity can generally normalize and control the experience. This low-anxiety approach to facilitating a lesson limits the opportunities students have to be at the center.

A third reason, and maybe the most prevalent factor that deters teachers from creating more learner-centered opportunities, is that asking students to move out of the familiar, sit-and-get approach to learning and into a more active role can cause some learners to struggle at first, particularly if they are not keen on the idea of carrying the responsibility that comes with driving the process. If the students aren't used to it, some will act out, get off task, socialize, or even lean into the learned-helplessness patterns that may have gotten other adults or peers to do their work for them in the past. While there will also be those who appreciate the opportunity and run with it, it's often the case that just as many may choose to disengage or waste time. If a teacher experiences that, can you blame them for being reluctant to do more of that type of learning in the future?

This creates a bit of a which-comes-first conundrum. Should our students' inability to self-regulate and learn on their own be a reason to avoid putting them in situations where they could foster the very skills they're lacking? Let me put it a different way. If we don't design learning opportunities that ask learners to develop the student agency and strategies necessary for them to drive their own learning, when will they ever learn how?

Despite all the reasons why creating learner-centered experiences can be challenging, it's work worth doing. But there's more to it than just having the opportunity. For personalization to have the desired positive impact on all learners, the students need to also possess the *ability* to capitalize on those opportunities by knowing how to drive their learning.

THE ABILITY

If learner-centered learning is the opportunity, then learner-driven learning speaks to the student's *ability in that moment* to drive the process. Think about it: As the teacher, I can design a learning experience where my students have the chance to be at the center, but if they don't have the know-how to move things forward, the experience will at best take a really long time, or at worst go nowhere and fail.

Each and every learner has the capacity to step into this role of leading their learning with agency and intentionality, but most need to be taught how. This step isn't as easy as it sounds because in practice the materials, the tools, and the strategies that each learner needs to employ to excel at this process may be different. Nonetheless, if teachers are not the ones teaching learners how to learn, then who is going to do it?

This is the step where personalization most commonly breaks down for one of a number of reasons. It could be that teachers instinctively do not believe that their students can handle being responsible for their learning (which is often correct, by the way). It might be that they trust their students enough to let them try, but when things inevitably get difficult for some and it falls apart, the teacher is never again as trusting. Some teachers contend that they don't have the time to teach learners how to learn (which makes some sense but also seems slightly ironic). And maybe the greatest hindrance to the development of learner-driven learning is that many educators struggle with teaching students how to conceptualize alternative ways of doing the work because they themselves have always taught utilizing the strategies that made the most sense to them.

Do not be discouraged by this. If you have ever felt this way or been deterred from trying something new because of similar feelings or challenges, the personalized practices in this book will help you persevere through these obstacles. Teaching learners how to learn is the real work of personalizing learning, and the decisions being made by the learners in the midst of that process are driven by the following list of drivers.

THE DRIVERS:
THE LEARNER'S STRENGTHS, PREFERENCES, INTERESTS, AND/OR NEEDS

If students are going to tailor the learning experience to suit them on an individual level, they will need to be taught some basic criteria that they can use to help them make decisions. This is where the language of *strengths, preferences, interests*, and *needs* from the definition comes into play.

Here's how it works. Let's say that a learner is given the opportunity to create a product of some sort that will display what they have learned. In that moment, the learner might decide to lean on their strength in writing and develop an essay that conveys what they know. Alternatively, let's pretend for a moment that this learner recently got the latest iPad and would prefer to use that device to record and produce a video that captures their learning. A third potential approach would be for the learner to create an analogy that compares a personal interest of theirs to the subject matter of this assignment (with little to no preference for capturing that in one medium versus another). Finally, it might be the case that the learner really needs to work on their writing skills, and as such, creates a writing piece to fulfill the requirements of this opportunity so that they can get additional practice and feedback as a writer. In each of these ways, what's driving the student's decision-making process is situationally different, and this component of the definition calls those differences to light through each of these four *drivers* for student decision-making when personalizing their learning.

CHAPTER 3

HOW TO PERSONALIZE LEARNING

THE ROLE OF CHOICE IN THE PERSONALIZATION OF LEARNING

Over the Memorial Day weekend of 2021, my family and I flew into San Francisco and went on a bit of a Northern California road trip to see Yosemite, Kings Canyon, and Sequoia National Parks. One afternoon during the trip, we were driving through Fresno in search of an authentic Mexican restaurant to stop at for lunch. After viewing at least fifteen different possibilities on Google, we found one that had a 4.8 rating after six-hundred-plus reviews, so we made our way to that location.

When we got there, we stepped inside and were met by the tantalizing smell of food being cooked on an open grill. After a full morning of hiking, we were all hungry. The meal options were posted on a sign above the counter, and I have no doubt that our collective gaze was quite comical as we searched to make meaning of a menu that was written entirely in Spanish. No one in our group knew how to read Spanish, but I saw the word *tacos* and knew what that meant, so I ordered three different tacos to try.

A few minutes later, my order was up. I went to the pickup window, grabbed my tacos, and sat down to enjoy them. The meat in the first one I did not recognize. The same was true for the second and the third. At that point, I took out my phone and entered the Spanish descriptors for each of the tacos I had ordered into Google Translate. Well, to my surprise, I had ordered the following: one cow's tongue taco, one intestinal meat taco, and the description of the third loosely translated to one "face meat" taco. I mustered up the courage to try each. One I liked, one I ate half of but found too greasy, and the third I didn't finish and would not order again. I left dissatisfied and still hungry.

Here's the thing. In that moment, I had the opportunity to make a decision. I had my choice of anything on the menu. I'm certain that there had to have been some delicious options on that board that I would have loved (and I'm sure the options I selected were options others enjoy). But I had no idea what I was doing, so I made an uninformed and rushed decision that did not work out in my favor.

Carrying this experience into an educational setting, I believe that our students, when given a choice in their learning, often make their decisions just as haphazardly as I did with the tacos. They search for the easiest option. They pick what their friends pick. They choose something that's familiar or maybe something at random. The point is that despite the fact that educators have been giving learners choices for years, when choice is leveraged for personalizing learning, there's a lot more to consider than is typically talked about with student choice.

In the last chapter, we looked at the definition for personalized learning and explored each of its three component parts in detail: the opportunity, the ability, and the drivers. In this chapter, we will pivot to considering the role that student choice plays across those three component parts. Viewing choice through the lens of personalization requires a deeper and broader understanding of how to implement student choice and the desired outcomes those experiences should produce. This is where we work on bringing the personalization of learning out of the theoretical realm, making it approachable and attainable for all teachers.

Adding Depth to How We Think About Learner Choice

Personalization asks that the learner be placed at the center with an opportunity and the ability to lead the learning, even if only for a moment. The easiest way to communicate and design for that moment is to think of it as a moment of choice. Student choice is that moment of learner-centered opportunity, but the question that follows is, Does the learner have the ability to make an academically sound decision when presented with that choice? This is where our conversation deviates from how we typically think about learner choice in education.

If we are going to expect learners to make strategic decisions, one choice at a time, we need to invest in the patient work of teaching them how to discover their strengths, preferences, interests, and needs (SPIN) and how to employ them on their own. It's students learning to put their own SPIN on their learning, and the process is as simple as asking our-selves a few questions: What options are available to the students? And what learning, information, or experiences might help empower them to make an informed decision? When implemented this way, there is such greater depth to how we leverage choice, and that depth makes learner-driven personalization possible.

What ends up being the case is that there are two distinctly different parts of this process. First, there's the period of time when the learners are acquiring the ability to make a given decision. Throughout this book we will refer to that scaffolding time frame and activities as *personalized practices*. Why? Well, because practice makes possible. What follows then is a distinctly different period of time when the learner has the actual opportunity to use what they gleaned from the personalized practice toward making a decision. That's the learner personalizing an aspect of their learning.

Okay, it's time for an example. And to set it up, I have a small confession to make: I am an English teacher, and I hate annotating. There, I said it. Please, don't judge.

Annotating a text is just not something I've ever really enjoyed. In high school, I tried the Post-it Note thing, but it always felt super clunky. You have to stop reading, pick up a pencil, and take notes on these tiny little Post-its that stick out of the book like the colored feathers of some failed Thanksgiving turkey craft.

Nope. Hard pass.

In college, I tried typing my annotations into a digital graphic organizer. It was an improvement, organizationally, but wow did that turn the experience of reading literature into something more akin to data entry.

Again, pass.

That's not to say that these strategies don't work for other people. I'm sure they do. But, they definitely do not work for me, and it wasn't until I started teaching that I found a solution to my problem.

BookSnaps.

In 2016, educator Tara M. Martin decided to turn her son's Snapchat app into an edu-tool by leveraging the phone's camera and the app's text and image overlays to create digital image-annotations that Tara coined as a *BookSnap*. The concept is pretty simple. When you find a quote or passage you would like to annotate, you use a device to take a picture of that quote on the page. Then you use an app, Snapchat in this case, to open and modify that image by underlining, circling, or highlighting the quote in some way. Finally, you add a layer of your own text, comments, and images over the photo that illustrates your thinking and interaction with the highlighted text.

After learning this strategy, I was hooked. To this day, I make sure to utilize my phone's camera anytime I'm reading, and I love organizing the images I create by adding them to a program like Padlet. Seriously, what a great idea; thanks, Tara!

Now, here's the good, the bad, and the moral of this story. The Good: I finally found an approach that works for me, and it's changed the way I think about annotating. The Bad: It took me until I was thirty-three years old to figure this out. The Moral: We can't allow optimal choices for student learning to go undiscovered during the K–12 experience.

Nearly every adult has a story similar to mine. We all have these "I wish I would have known . . . " stories that point to a time when we learned something about how we learn best but did so far too late in life. We can address this in K–12 education by amplifying our efforts with teaching kids how to learn, which we can do by thinking more deeply about how we might utilize student choice for personalizing learning.

Now for the example: Having learned about BookSnaps, I decided that the next time I asked my students to annotate, I was going to design a personalized practice to teach them a variety of ways to annotate and that they should use that experience to identify a strategy that works best for them. My thought was to lead this personalized practice during the first half of the novel, and that way, by the back half of the book, the learners could have the opportunity to personalize their learning by using the strategy that worked best for them.

The personalized practice went something like this:

For the sake of conversation, let's say the novel was divided into ten readings that were assigned to be read over three weeks' time. Prior to the first reading, we devoted three minutes to establishing what we were doing by annotating and why we were doing it. During that conversation, I communicated that there are many different ways of annotating, and that we would be conducting a personalized practice, an experiment of sorts, to see which of three approaches to annotating they individually *preferred*.

Next step, same day. We spent five minutes learning how to annotate using Post-its. We established what to write, how to assign different colors to different topics, how to place the Post-its around the edges, etc.

Having had that conversation, the expectation was that every student annotate on Post-its for reading one.

Fast-forward to day two. I made it a point to check annotations, so that learners could revise their work if it wasn't meeting our expectations. Once everyone had received feedback, we devoted another five minutes to discussing how to annotate, but this time, we talked about the benefits of recording annotations on a digital graphic organizer. Then, you guessed it, students used a digital graphic organizer to annotate during reading two.

On day three, more of the same: annotation check, feedback, and a third five-minute session, this time on BookSnaps, which became the required annotation style for reading three.

After three rounds of personalized practice, that was it for the scaffolding. However, you could elect to teach a fourth annotation strategy if you have one, or you could potentially double back and require one more round of exposure to each strategy over the course of readings four, five, and six—just to make sure that learners have enough information to choose with confidence. Teachers, the number of strategies you teach and the amount of repetition you offer learners as a part of the personalized practice phase is entirely up to you. Remember that teaching is an art, so look to design, adapt, and redesign any of the personalized practices in this book according to what you believe is in the best interest of your learners' development.

Keeping the end goal in mind, phase two requires that we empower our learners with the freedom to choose to annotate in whatever way they believe works best for them. Learners were given complete control over the annotation strategy that they used. In just under three weeks' time, each learner had developed an annotation preference that they believed in, that they could communicate, and that they could use when given the opportunity to do so in the future, because they now had the ability, thanks to the personalized practice experience, to choose wisely.

Note the clear distinction in the example between the two phases: the personalized practice and the opportunity for the learner to personalize their annotation strategy. The personalized practice was teacher-led, whole-group conversations and a systematic approach to learning about, and experimenting with, each strategy, one at a time, together. It took several days to conduct that personalized practice, but it was critical toward making sure that each learner had the ability to drive their process when the opportunity presented itself. When it did, the learners personalized their learning the moment they had the opportunity to choose. That would have looked like each learner independently utilizing their preferred annotation strategy, simultaneously and forever moving forward.

There will be those who challenge this approach, citing that there might be an infinite number of ways to annotate, and as such, it's impossible to find the *ideal* match for each student. That's a fair argument, but I guess I'm just more of a cup-half-full kind of guy. To me, this just tripled the number of options students previously had, and what's more, it communicated to them loud and clear that alternative strategies exist, and finding better ones for you can make learning easier, more effective, and at times even fun. That's a win in my book.

There will also be those who push back, questioning if personalizing annotations really qualifies as personalizing learning. I can see that point but want to encourage you to read on, as the next chapter will stretch our thinking beyond adding depth to choice and into a conversation about how to broaden our understanding of where these types of choice opportunities might be possible.

Adding Breadth to the Way We Think About Learner Choice

After school each day, I try to sneak over to our school's weight room to get a quick workout in before I head home. I'm not the only educator at our school who does this, and one afternoon as I was finishing up on the treadmill, a teacher friend of mine walked up to chat.

"Andrew," he said, "I've been thinking about doing some sort of personalized thing with my class, and, well, the trouble I'm having is that the stuff we are doing, there's really only one way to do it. That's it. There's not a whole lot of choice in it, ya know? The kids either know how to do it or they don't, and I can't just let them create whatever they want, because the indicator we are working on is looking for a specific skill that they are supposed to demonstrate. So, yeah; I want to do some personalizing, but I don't think it'll work with what I teach."

The issue expressed in this conversation is one of the most common concerns I hear when working with teachers around personalization. I have to admit, my friend's point here is valid; he's stuck and not from a lack of interest or effort. It was clearly on his mind—he sought me out to talk about it!

In life, it's often the case that what we see is limited to what we look for, and my friend's narrow perspective on choice prevented him from seeing all the instructional changes he could potentially make! In his mind, *choice* could only mean that students would have a say in how they demonstrated their learning, and given the content and standards he was teaching, there wasn't room for learner choice in that particular part of the process. This left him frustrated and stumped.

In every lesson, activity, or unit lies the opportunity to provide learners with a choice, but we have to think flexibly enough to see it. For example, some teachers offer their learners a choice in what they can read for class. Others give students a choice over the activities or assignments that they are being asked to do. Student choice can be found in due dates, project ideas, materials, or even in aspects of the learning like where a student chooses to sit. To be able to broaden our vision and see where choice is possible, we need to know specifically where to look. Ask yourself, what are some of the typical steps that are characteristic of most learning experiences?

Below is a list of seven notably different aspects of the learning process. We will explore each of these, individually, in the chapters that follow.

- Topic
- Instructional Delivery
- Learning Strategies
- Product (Assessment)
- Pace
- Communication
- Learning Space

Presenting each step of the learning in this way allows us to see the full breadth of where we might look to offer learners a choice within a learning experience. In any lesson, activity, or unit there will always be at least one opportunity to infuse student choice. It's just a matter of front-loading with a personalized practice. And yes, similar to my friend's situation, it's also likely that there will be one or more areas where choice simply doesn't make sense, and that's okay.

Remember, *fully personalized* is not the goal, but as our content changes over the course of the year, we should be consistently aiming to do two things: afford learners the power to continue to drive scenarios where they already have the ability to do so, and be proactive in designing new personalized practices as scaffolding for any upcoming choice opportunities.

Instead of striving for a fully personalized experience, aim to fully saturate any lesson, activity, or unit with as many choice opportunities as the learning allows and the learners are prepared to handle. Doing this asks each learner to take on an ever-increasing amount of academic responsibility, but that transfer is gradual and carefully supported. That's how to design learner-driven personalized learning.

A CLOSING NOTE

Never forget that your role as a teacher is only enhanced by this work. While the students will be taking on some of what you may have once felt was your responsibility, that only frees you up to amplify the impact you can have as an expert resource, a learning coach, a personalized practice designer, and most importantly, as an adult who sees them, who listens, who responds, and who clearly cares about setting them up for lifelong success.

CHAPTER 4

FOUR STRATEGIES THAT SUPPORT PERSONALIZED PRACTICES

In this chapter, we will briefly discuss four of the go-to instructional strategies that frequently play a role in (or work in support of) a personalized practice. Front-loading these now will equip you with the knowledge necessary to understand their integration into the ideas we will explore in the rest of the book.

PL DESIGN STRATEGY #1: ADMINISTER A PRETEST

A pretest is an assessment that a teacher can administer prior to the start of a lesson, activity, or unit that informs both the teacher and the learners of what they already know and what they don't know about the topic as the learning for that experience begins.

Historically, when pretests are given, it's the teacher who ends up being the one using the data from the results to refine the instruction and to potentially create ability groups for differentiation. But once again, this is *the teacher* doing the heavy lifting of reading the data and modifying the experiences as a result.

Personalized learning seeks to empower *the learner* with this same data, and a personalized practice would be to teach learners about the role this information can play in their decision-making process. For example, when a score on an indicator is strong, that signals a *strength*, and conversely, if the score for a particular indicator is weak, that signals a *need* for the learner. In this way, the pretest reveals two of the factors that we have already identified as drivers of the student's decision-making. Armed with this information, the learner possesses the ability to make a data-informed decision, but as always, the student will need an opportunity to reference and use this data as they make a decision. In the chapters that follow, we will reference pretests or pre-assessments often and how they might be best support student decision-making.

PL DESIGN STRATEGY #2: DEVELOP A LEARNER-INTEREST INVENTORY

To keep it real, this is just a fancy way to say a survey. Learner-Interest Inventories are a series of questions that will bring to light some of the interests and current preferences that a learner may possess at the beginning of the year, or semester, or unit. In this way, it functions similarly to a pretest in that it produces two of the four drivers that can inform the learner's decision-making. However, think of it as a snapshot and not something carved in stone because interests and preferences can change.

A question I'm often asked is, What questions should I ask students in a Learner-Interest Inventory? The best advice I can give is to say that you should not ask a question unless the answer will directly help the learner make a decision about a choice they are being offered. For example, what good is it to ask students what their favorite color is if there's no opportunity for them to later access that info and apply it as they create something colorful?

The process instead should go as follows. Identify what choice(s) the students will have available to them in their future learning. Then design the personalized practice(s) that would serve as scaffolding in support of those decisions. As you do this, write down any questions whose answers might serve as a sort of pre-brainstorming set that could spark ideas or support the personalized practice or the decision in the moment of choice itself. Turn those questions into a short, pointed survey, and there's your Learner-Interest Inventory. Administer it, and once the results are in, find a way for learners to have consistent and easy access to that information for the time when it is most pertinent to their process.

It's important to point out that a Learner-Interest Inventory is *not* a personality test. There is a real temptation here to administer a survey that will designate each student as being of a certain *learner type*, but I would advise against such assessments. While well intended, these surveys can do more harm than good. They put students in a box by assigning both strengths and weaknesses to each learner that may or may not be true. Carrying the weight of that label, both the positives and the negatives, can be burdensome and even defeating for kids.

Again, a Learner-Interest Inventory is mentioned here so we can quickly reference it, where applicable, later. If you're still interested in specific questions or an example for various grade levels, check out some of the sample surveys on my website at AndrewDEaston.com.

PL DESIGN STRATEGY #3: DO NOT DEVELOP A PERSONAL LEARNER PROFILE

Nearly every educator invested in personalizing learning talks about Personal Learner Profiles (or PLPs for short) as if they are the holy grail of personalization. If the concept of a PLP is new to you, think of it as an IEP (individualized education plan) for every student. It's essentially a digital backpack of student information and data that would travel with the learner from grade to grade or teacher to teacher. Personalization enthusiasts dream of PLPs that house information for all four drivers in one place, along with a portfolio of students' past work and, in some instances, a complete list of students' goals and/or progress with various competencies.

While the value of such a piece would seem inherent, a PLP is a great idea in theory that does not translate over into practice. It just doesn't work, and there are several reasons why. First, learner preferences and interests can change over time, with new experiences, new technology, and an increased sensitivity on the learner's part to the conditions that they need to be at their best. As such, some students will frequently need to update the info in the PLP for their drivers. This can become tedious and time consuming. It's also not something that's easily facilitated as a whole class because there will be variability in the frequency with which learners need to record changes. Frankly, it can be hard enough to get students to put their names on their papers and to turn in their assignments on time; imagine the challenge of getting them to consistently update their PLPs as well.

Second, the drivers of learning can be influenced by a number of factors. I'll use my daughter as an example. At home she likes to do her math at the table but prefers to read on the couch. So if she's asked to enter into the PLP her preferred place to do work, what should she say? Additionally, I've had students say that they prefer to learn collaboratively, but they recognize that the subject area or their friend group in a given class significantly impacts the effectiveness of that preference. Not to mention that there are moments when we all simply need to work alone. The point here is that the drivers can be situational and incredibly nuanced.

Finally, an effective PLP would need to be robust enough to house a substantial amount of student info, while also being practical enough to support learners during a personalized practice or in their moment of choice. If students have to open a program and dive eighteen clicks deep to access the information needed to help them make a decision, they're just not going to use it, which defeats the whole purpose of the PLP in the first place.

While I can appreciate what a PLP would represent, it's impractical. Instead, stick to administering pretests and Learner-Interest Inventories that are targeted at equipping learners with the info they need to drive their decisions in their upcoming learning.

PL DESIGN STRATEGY #4:
DEVELOP A COMMUNICATION LOOP FOR
TEACHER CLARITY AND FEEDBACK

In order for any of these personalized practices to be effective, the teacher must strive for clarity in communicating the *why*, *how*, and *what* behind each personalized practice and its subsequent learner-driven choice opportunity.

The following list captures the conversation markers that should take place at some point as a teacher facilitates this process.

- Before initiating a personalized learning experience in your class or course, teach students what personalized learning is and how this type of learning can benefit them.
- With each new choice, teach students about the decision they will be able to make and preview the options they will eventually have. Discuss which drivers might be relevant to that decision.
- Take the time to teach learners the pros and cons of each choice as it is presented to the students (when it's applicable). This is best done as a reflective conversation led by the learners after having had a chance to experience the choice for themselves.
- Whenever you can, provide positive verbal feedback, individually or publicly, as learners demonstrate their agency by

making strategic decisions with the opportunities for choice that they have.

- Facilitate an end-of-the-lesson/activity/unit survey that forces students to reflect. Such a survey will also capture learner feedback that can impact your future personalized practice design.
- Always share with the class what you are learning from the experience and how their input, actions, inactions, etc. are constantly shaping how you teach, lead, and facilitate the experience.

The point here is not to overthink any one of these conversations but to create a classroom culture where this type of thinking and conversation is clear, ever present, and something that the learner grasps and can articulate. In this way, the teacher is modeling, through conversation and brief activities, the metacognitive process that goes into being an effective and reflective learner. Expect this process to be necessary for every new choice and personalized practice you implement. As you read on, understand that these conversations are taking place across all of the learner choice options made available.

CHAPTER 5

LEARNER CHOICE
IN TOPIC

This is the first of seven chapters that each explore the opportunity for learner choice in a different aspect of the learning process. In every chapter, expect an initial explanation of that facet, followed by a list of classroom-tested examples of choice. Also anticipate reading about the personalized practices that would precede the choice and teach learners how to put their own SPIN on that opportunity. As you read, your goal should be to learn and then think deeply about where and how you might make a similar choice available for your students. Then design backward, considering what personalized practices might help scaffold learners' ability to make decisions about choice on their own.

Okay, let's dive into thinking about learner choice in topic. The first thing we need to be clear about here is that *topic* and *content* are not exactly synonymous. *Content* is the information and materials your team, department, school, or district is expecting you to teach or use. Delivering your assigned content is typically nonnegotiable, so understand that when we talk about choice in *topic*, we are not talking about audibling out of the *content* you are required to teach.

There's a common misconception that personalized learning is this Montessori-style approach to public education where students can spend their time learning about whatever they want.

That's simply not the case.

And yet, there are times in education when the skill being developed is more important than the subject matter of the text or the topic being discussed to foster that skill. Take K–2 reading materials, for example. My son brings home these little paper readers that have titles like *A Fat Cat* and *The Wish for Fish* where the focus is clearly on the act of reading itself, the level of the words used, and the repetitive sounds embedded in those words. The topic of those stories is secondary at best.

But just because that's common practice does not mean that it's best practice. Student interest is a powerful piece that can be leveraged to drive a learner's investment in their academic growth. More importantly, what is learning if not the satiation of the thirst for new knowledge, to satisfy a curiosity? As such, isn't it our job as practitioners to teach our kids how to tune into the things that may fascinate them, if they are only thoughtful enough to look a little closer?

Learner choice in topic matters.

So, let's not overlook the fact that most learners, when given the choice to choose their own topic, have little to no idea how to make that kind of decision. The passive "it sounded kinda good" isn't good enough.

Therefore, when it makes sense, design personalized practices that help students develop an approach to how they make a choice-in-topic decision.

EXAMPLES OF WHERE LEARNER CHOICE IN TOPIC IS POSSIBLE

Let's begin by first recognizing where this type of choice might exist within what you currently teach. Here's are some examples of scenarios where there might be an opportunity for choice in topic.

- **SOCIAL STUDIES:** Any opportunity learners have to research a historical figure, an event, an era, a city, a country, etc. of their choice.
- **SOCIAL STUDIES:** Any inquiry activity where answering an essential question is more important than regurgitation of the facts of any specific era or event in history. In these instances, any past event is a potential example, leaving room for learner choice in topic.
- **PERFORMING ARTS:** Allow students to select a piece or performance to evaluate, emulate, or perform.
- **PSYCHOLOGY:** If the content for a unit is fixed on one thematic topic, let's say *sleep and dreams*, there could be a common shared text for all learners, while individually, students could also be expected to become experts on a subtopic of their choosing (i.e., a specific sleep disorder). Note that there's the potential to follow up with the jigsaw strategy here.
- **PHYSICAL EDUCATION:** Students might be asked to research any sport or athlete.
- **SOCIOLOGY:** Students select one culturally relevant detail about a people group to study. Again, with the potential to jigsaw.
- **MATH:** Students might have options in the narratives they choose to read for story problems.
- **MATH:** Students might use pretest data to determine what concepts they already know versus the ones they need to learn or revisit, which would afford them choice in the topics they learn about based upon their need.
- **SCIENCE:** At the end of a series of lessons or units, students might be given the chance to select a concept to revisit and delve deeper into through additional readings.
- **SCIENCE:** Students could select a natural phenomenon to research, discuss, and analyze according to a set of criteria or methods.

- **PROJECT-BASED LEARNING (PBL) AND COMMUNITY-BASED LEARNING (CBL):** The focus for either of these learning experiences is developed by the learners to serve a purpose, meet a need, etc. As such, the topic is often discovered by the students through the development of a driving question and pursued as they seek to answer it.
- **FOODS:** Students might take part in a dessert challenge that allows them to select a recipe of their choice to prepare.
- **SPEECH OR ESSAY WRITING:** Students are often given a choice in the topic on which they center their report.

While there will be times when choice in topic doesn't make sense given your content or standards, it's also clear that choice in topic is possible across a variety of grade levels and content areas. In fact, most classroom teachers reading this list will likely have given their students a choice-in-topic opportunity before, which might mean that right now you are questioning if reading this chapter is necessary.

Well, before you decide to skip ahead, remember that our aim is to think more deeply about choice.

I often hear educators say, "Well, I personalize practically everything now, so thanks, but I'm already doing this." In these moments, educators confuse giving learners a choice with the act of teaching students how to make a decision. Those are very different things. The first focuses only on the opportunity, where the latter is committed to fostering learner agency and self-efficacy.

With all seven of these conversations regarding where choice is possible, there will be the temptation to stop short and take choice at face value, but remember to ask yourself what measures are in place to ensure that all learners have the ability to make an intelligent decision when given the opportunity to choose. If the answer to that is, "Well, I told them that they could choose whatever they wanted," then we still have some work to do.

DEVELOPING PERSONALIZED PRACTICES
FOR LEARNER CHOICE IN TOPIC

Getting to this step means that you have seen an opportunity for students to make a choice-in-topic decision in your class or course, and now you're ready to design your own personalized practice to teach them how they might make that kind of decision.

As you begin thinking through that design, you will be tempted to create options *for* the students. Whether that's a list of potential speech or research topics, a curated set of novels, or a collection of articles that you make available, it will feel like the right thing to do. And while that thought is in no way misguided, I would encourage you to table that idea for now. Instead, recognize that the person who is doing the work is doing the learning. There is an opportunity here for students to create or curate their own options, but most of them will not be able to do this without your support. It's here, in that space between the ideal and the struggles of our current reality, where we find the teachable moment that personalized practices address.

So instead, ask yourself, What would I do to develop a list of options here? and, How can I teach my students to handle that responsibility?

There are a myriad of ways a teacher could go about designing a learning experience to address these questions. Keep that in mind as we nail personalization down to the practical level of implementation. The examples shared are one way to accomplish the desired outcome, but they are certainly not the only way. They represent the thinking that's driving this work and model some strategies that can be used or modified as a means to that end.

Speaking specifically to how learners might navigate a choice in topic, there are two factors that should be considered when creating an option: student interest and the requirements of the standard or skill being assessed. We can address the student interest piece by embedding some specific questions into a Learner-Interest Inventory. Doing so will create a brainstorming list that students can reference and draw inspiration from when asked to choose.

For example, if students are developing a speech, the Learner-Interest Inventory may have previously asked questions like, What are three things you nerd-out about? or, What are three talents that you have that people might not know you possess? You might also write a question more specific to the prompt. So if learners will be asked to deliver a report on a noteworthy person, ask a question like, If you could have dinner with any three people alive or dead, who would you invite?

As you craft these questions, keep this advice in mind.

1. Have learners complete the inventory well in advance of the moment they need that info for their decision. It's often that students shut down when brainstorming with a prompt in front of them. Answering these questions days or weeks beforehand expedites the process, both for the learner and the teacher in support of the student. The ideas are already there.

2. When a question is open ended, ask for a minimum of three responses. Force students to dig past the most immediate, surface-level answers. Plus, having several to pick from also gives them ideas to shoot down later, which is important when it comes to brainstorming.

3. While not every question can be worded in an interesting way, try to phrase things as uniquely as you can. For example, I could have asked for three people who you find interesting or three people who inspire you, but the phrasing of inviting them to dinner is quirky and slightly more thought provoking.

So to address the student interest portion of this choice-in-topic decision, the personalized practice may involve teaching the students, as a whole class and later individually, to reference their Learner-Interest Inventory to mine for ideas.

Ideas, plural.

Again, you'll be tempted here to revert back to just letting them pick the topic from their survey that sounds good. Instead, ask students to bring not one but two or three options out of the idea-dig and into the evaluation phase of this potential personalized practice. The real work here is to teach them how to weigh each possible topic according to the second part we mentioned earlier: the requirements of the task at hand.

The support here would be to create a topic evaluation form, basically a handout with a blank grid on it, where students could list potential topics across the top and evaluation criteria down the left-hand side. You can find an example of this form on my website.

What goes into the criteria?

Well, why don't you ask the students.

Ask the students, when they have the prompt and rubric in hand, to point out the three to four key requirements of the assignment that the topic needs to address. Together discuss and model how to tease out those must-have elements, and then support students as they evaluate each of *their* two to three topics according to the criteria that *they* highlighted. Again, for an example of this, access the videos that accompany the form at AndrewDEaston.com.

Teacher clarity and involvement here is paramount. This is not handing out an evaluation form and sitting at your desk. It's not allocating five minutes for the students to complete it, silently, on their own. It's also not enough to simply lead the students through the form by reading the directions aloud. It's teaching them that thoughtful brainstorming matters, and that the things they care about can be academic if they only look at them through a different lens. It's bringing the whole class together to learn a process that they can build upon and apply as they pursue their curiosities and passions in the future. Seize the opportunity to lead.

Now, you may be saying, "Wait, how is this personalized?"

Personalized practices seek to teach the type of thinking that learners can later use to personalize their own process. The goal is not the personalization of the practice; it's for the practice to empower the learner to have the ability to personalize thereafter.

Key word here: *thereafter.*

So having navigated this practice opportunity, find a way to put them back in this situation again, and when you do, remove yourself from the process. You might think of this as a gradual release from "I do" to "we do" through "you do." Just remind them of the personalized practice they went through previously and have them submit a justification for the idea they select. Be their coach, but recognize that in that moment it's game time, so capitalize on what's been practiced and entrust them with the opportunity to play.

Here, we've taught the learner how to own the work that we so often do ourselves as educators, curating ideas. Over time, we can go even deeper by having students develop the prompt, the rubric criteria, or both. A student who is able to do this well has developed a skill that will serve them well as a lifelong learner, but they have to be taught how to navigate the opportunity to pursue a topic.

MAKING A CHOICE-IN-TOPIC DECISION FROM A STUDENT'S PERSPECTIVE

Jalen is a sophomore. He's a bright student who is good at math and science and is content with getting a B in English class. Jalen generally dislikes reading. His comprehension skills are fine, it's just that he's so detail oriented that it's made him a slow reader.

Impatient and often disinterested, Jalen habitually opts to read SparkNotes or browse through Reddit or Amazon book reviews instead of actually reading the whole-class novels he's assigned. Then in class, he listens closely to the discussions about the book and gleans just enough information to speak broadly about the events of the text. That experience, coupled with his natural ability, is typically good enough to earn him a B, which only affirms this behavior.

Well, that worked until one teacher flipped the process on its head.

That was the day that the students were told that they could select whatever book they wanted to read. Now, there were some criteria that had to be met. Jalen's teacher noted that it needed to be a piece of non-fiction, over two hundred pages long, and each student was expected to submit a justification for the book they chose.

Jalen was intrigued by this unexpected wrinkle in the familiar rhythm of how the whole read-a-novel process typically goes, but at the same time he was nervous because he didn't know what he would do if he couldn't just sit back and borrow ideas from his peers who had actually read the book.

Jalen's thoughts were cut short as the teacher instructed them to take out their Learner-Interest Inventory. Looking specifically at questions three, eleven, and twenty-one, they were to write down four things they were passionate about. Jalen had always loved basketball, action movies, indie music, and building things with his hands, so he recorded those from his survey.

Then, the teacher started a discussion that Jalen initially did not have any clue how to respond to.

"What is something quirky that you appreciate about some books over others?" Jalen's teacher asked the class.

There was a moment of uncomfortable silence.

Then one student spoke up and said they liked it when a book had a larger font because it made the book easier to see. That made it more enjoyable for her to read. Another commented that she felt long chapters were defeating, and so she preferred books with shorter chapters because getting through them gave her momentum and a sense of accomplishment.

Jalen was intrigued by the conversation. He had never considered these ideas before.

The preferences kept pouring in. Some liked large margins. Some said they preferred owning their own copy so that they could write in the book. This conversation went on for several minutes before the teacher asked the class to write down three personal preferences that they have about books.

Jalen noted that he preferred short chapters, big fonts on small pages, and books as short as possible.

Once everyone had finished jotting down their preferences, the teacher asked the students to access a document that had been shared via their learning management system (LMS). That doc listed over 250 nonfiction titles. Each title was accompanied by one to three words that shared the general topics addressed in the text and a link to the book listing on Amazon.

At the teacher's request, Jalen started to go through the list looking for books that matched any of the interests he had written down. In the first page alone he found three, and so he clicked on the link for each and started to look at the Amazon listing.

His teacher had pointed out what Jalen had already known to do, read the reviews. But what he hadn't done before was look at the picture of the book's pages to see if he liked the layout of the words on the page.

In the end, Jalen found not only a nonfiction text that he thought he might like but also a book formatted in a way he appreciated. The shared doc noted that there was a copy of the book in the school library, so Jalen checked it out.

That night, Jalen went home and read the first fifteen pages of the book . . . and he hated it.

The author wrote in really long sentences that Jalen found difficult to read. Thankfully, his teacher had said that if anyone didn't like their book, they should come in and discuss making another selection. So that's what Jalen did.

"What did you not like about the book?" his teacher asked.

"The way the author writes is really long, and, I don't know, that kinda messed me up," Jalen explained.

"That's fine," the teacher said. "I think that happens to most avid readers. You get ten to twenty pages in and go, yeah, this is not for me. So what did you learn?"

"That I don't like it when people write like that."

"So, why don't you go back to the list, look through a few more options, and when you find one you might like, read a paragraph or two in the preview on Amazon before you make your decision."

"Wait. Were we supposed to do that?" asked Jalen with a blank look on his face.

His teacher offered a wry smile and simply nodded yes.

Jalen went on to make another selection. This time he picked his book based on the topic, the layout, and the author's writing style. Even though the text was 287 pages long, it was the first book Jalen had ever finished reading, cover to cover, for school.

That's how Jalen learned to personalize his approach to selecting the things he is interested in reading. Today, some of his preferences have broadened or changed, but Jalen always has a process, a plan that's his own, and it's changed the way he thinks about reading.

CHAPTER 6

LEARNER CHOICE IN INSTRUCTIONAL DELIVERY

A more accurate way to talk about this choice would be to call it learner choice in instructional delivery modality, but that's quite a mouthful, and maybe it's an overly complicated way of saying that there are different mediums through which an individual can learn.

Having this conversation was much more challenging for educators to wrap their minds around prior to the online learning that took place during the COVID-19 pandemic. A silver lining from the hardships of that time is that today, teachers everywhere have the tech skills to deliver instruction in ways other than lecturing. Now the focus can be on how those lessons learned might further our efforts in support of personalizing learning.

The universality of this particular choice cannot be overemphasized. No matter the grade level or subject area, we all lead through direct instruction at times. As such, this particular choice is often possible even when no other options may seem to exist. (Yes, I'm talking to you, math teachers.)

As you read, stay open and think flexibly about what instructional time can look like.

Examples of Where Learner Choice in Instructional Delivery Is Possible

Once we identify what choices are possible, we can work backward from there. Here's a list of potential avenues through which students can learn. Keep in mind, this is not an exhaustive set of examples. This list will continue to grow with this work and with each new technological advancement.

- In-person lectures and direct instruction
- Instructional videos
- Podcasts or audio files
- Hard-copy reading materials, textbooks, handouts, etc.
- Digital reading materials, textbooks, articles, etc.
- Hyperdocs
- Instruction from a peer and/or peer feedback
- Web pages and blog sites
- Slide decks
- Social media posts and stories
- A digital copy being read aloud in the student's preferred language via a text-to-speech voice reader
- Augmented reality experiences
- Virtual reality experiences
- Live video conferencing: lectures, panels, webinars, etc.
- Direct instruction from artificial intelligence
- The combination of two or more of these choices, creating a multimodal resource
- . . . and more. The possibilities here are truly endless.

The majority of these options are familiar to teachers. Most educators will have used several of them, situationally, before. However, it's rare to hear of two, three, four, or more modalities being used simultaneously. It's rarer still for multiple modes to be leveraged as student-choice options.

So, just to be clear, this is not a conversation about flipped videos. It's also not a conversation about how to deliver assignment directions at non-teacher-led stations in a blended learning, station-rotation model. What we are talking about here is learners developing their own SPIN on what instructional modalities they choose to access in a way that is both strategic and situational.

Amassing Instructional Delivery Options and the Conditions for Their Implementation

If our learners are going to have the freedom to learn from a lecture, a textbook, a video, or a slide deck, the question becomes fairly obvious: Where do I, as the teacher, begin? And the answer, of course, is amassing options.

Yes—I'm aware that this goes against everything we discussed in the previous chapter about not creating options *for* the students. But this choice is different. Learners receive instruction as a way to access knowledge that is outside of their current experiences and understanding. This means the information must come from somewhere or someone other than the student. And while a learner could create a video or deliver instruction to their peers, that would be a demonstration of learner choice in product, which is a conversation for a later chapter.

So again, the first step is to amass options. You will want to be thoughtful about this. Take some time to think through which modalities you (or your team) would like to make available. As you do that work, here are three factors to keep in mind.

1. **THE SCOPE:** For how many lessons will this choice be an option for students?
2. **THE CONTENT CURRENTLY AVAILABLE:** How many new pieces will you need to find or create?
3. **THE TIME FRAME:** How much time do you have to develop or pull these resources together?

Preparing to offer three choices for five lessons obviously requires less prep work than four choices for ten. Set a manageable goal and grow from there. Personalized practices also empower the teacher to design the practice according to where they are.

For the sake of conversation, let's say that we would like to offer learners their choice of three instructional delivery modalities, specifically direct instruction, a recorded video lesson, and a hard-copy, typed-out version of that instruction the students can read independently.

Let's also pretend that your team has agreed to offer these options for each of the five instruction-heavy lessons in a unit that's a little over a month away.

If none of these materials have been made or curated yet, your team will have some work to do. If that sounds like a lot, I'm not going to lie, it can be. But trust me when I say that it's totally worth it. I was always better teaching live after I had spent some thoughtful time creating alternative instructional content. Plus, preparing these pieces in advance meant that once the unit started, I wasn't taking home lesson planning, which was always a nice mental reprieve.

For time-saving tips and tricks for how to develop these pieces with efficiency and fidelity, check out the video on "Creating Multiple Instructional Modalities" on AndrewDEaston.com.

Creating the options is half of the prep; the other is designing the implementation. That means developing a personalized practice. So here are a few questions worth considering as you get started.

- Will every student be required to access each instructional lesson, or can students use their pretest scores to test out of certain content?
- Is it the expectation that students utilize just one modality, or are you designing the experience with the hope that they engage several?

- Should the content of each instructional piece be identical, or is it okay if the different resources take a slightly different look at the information being conveyed?

There's no right or wrong way to answer these questions, but those answers will significantly impact the scaffolding process and overall student experience for this choice.

To fully play out our hypothetical scenario, let's imagine that we would like for our three modalities to all convey the same information. That means the students would only need to engage one of the three modes. And if their pretest scores indicate that they know the information, we are not going to ask them to go through instruction for that specific piece of content.

Developing Personalized Practices for Learner Choice in Instructional Delivery

With the choices created and the conditions in place, we can now design the personalized practice. In our example scenario, we've got approximately one month to prepare our learners to make a sound decision when the choice for instructional modality is made available.

One approach here would be to give students the chance to experience each modality, one at a time, to help them develop a preference. To do this well, teacher clarity is key. Devote at least five minutes to a whole-class conversation about what instruction is and what constitutes a modality. Then be transparent about what the personalized practices will aim to foster. They might identify a strength, make known a preference, allow a student to bring their interest in a modality into their learning, or highlight how one modality is problematic for a student, a need for an alternative or supplement if only that one modality is offered.

Following that chat, the next time you would normally deliver whole-class instruction, explicitly point out that this is the instructional time and that, in this case, the instruction is being delivered through direct instruction. Ask the class or point out positives, like the learner's ability to ask questions, and drawbacks, such as the student's inability to control the pace. Then teach as you normally would.

As soon as your instruction is finished, administer a short survey that asks three to five comprehension questions over the material you just taught. End that survey with an open-ended opportunity for the students to record their opinions on direct instruction as a way to learn. Save the survey results in a place that students can easily access their own answers in the future.

When it becomes instructional time again (the next day or days later), replicate the same process but for a different modality. Let's say it's video instruction this time. Acknowledge that it's instructional time, note that the delivery modality is video, discuss the benefits and drawbacks of video as a learning mode, and then let the whole class access the video, independently, learning as they go. When the video is finished, administer a similar survey and log the results with the others.

Then replicate this process for the third modality, a hard-copy, typed-out text.

While one rotation through every option is good, making it through all three, twice, would be better. Again, practice makes possible. Before long, students will have the experience and the data they need to make an intelligent decision when they are empowered to choose their instructional modality.

Making a Choice in Instructional Delivery from a Student's Perspective

Shivani is an eighth grader who has always found it hard to pay attention in class. When her teachers talk, her mind begins to wander. By the time her attention returns, the conversation has moved so far ahead that she feels lost. If it weren't for the helpful support of her friends in and outside of class, she would really struggle.

This disjointed routine changed for Shivani when her science teacher started to teach using personalized practices for choice in instructional modalities.

"It was weird at first," Shivani recalled. "I was like, why are we learning this stuff, because we're students, and it's not like I don't know that teachers talk a lot. That's kinda the job, right? But, the more we talked about it, it surprised me because I had never really thought about how I learn. At least not that much."

Shivani learned the benefits and drawbacks of different modalities. She got to try out several of them and give her opinion on what worked for her and what didn't. The whole process taught Shivani some things that really surprised her.

"We took these little quiz/survey things after every instruction time," Shivani explained, "and mine told me that I learn best from reading, and I was like, that can't be right, because I'm not a fast reader. But after a couple of times trying it, I was like, okay, I'm getting this now. And yeah . . . it was working better."

Reading kept Shivani actively engaged. It also gave her control over the pace of her learning. So when she had the option to choose what mode to learn through, Shivani chose to read. But then, something odd happened.

Before the start of instructional time, the teacher always passed out the readings before starting the direct instruction, which meant Shivani would be several paragraphs in before the small-group lecture commenced in the corner of the room. Once that started, Shivani found her attention drawn to the lecture and away from her reading. But this time, it made more sense to her because the reading gave her the context for the conversation.

That's when Shivani had an idea. She decided to approach her teacher with a question.

"Could I maybe get a copy of the reading early?" she asked.

"I don't see why not," her teacher responded, "but what are you going to do during the instructional time in class if you've already gone through it before?"

"Well, when I was sitting over there today I realized that reading ahead helped me to not get lost when you were speaking. I'm thinking I should try to read before class and then just go to your lecture group because asking questions has always helped, and I still want to be able to do that."

And that's how Shivani learned to personalize how she receives instruction.

CHAPTER 7

LEARNER CHOICE IN LEARNING STRATEGY

I once worked with a team of two science teachers who could not have been more different, as people and as practitioners. Despite their contrasting styles, they were both highly effective as teachers, and generally speaking, they worked well with one another.

The two had been on this particular team for twelve years, and apparently when they first started working together they had engaged in a series of embittered battles over the right way to teach certain concepts. As professionals, they worked it out, agreeing to disagree on some things. And they moved forward with the unspoken agreement that, despite delivering common summative assessments, each of them would teach their students to solve certain problems or complete processes the way that made the most sense to them.

Tasked with helping this team work together on developing some personalized practices for their course, it seemed to me perfect to bring their differing perspectives together for a choice-in-strategy experience.

Treading lightly, I was able to coax these passionate practitioners into experimenting with teaching not only their own preferred approach, but also using their counterpart's methods for solving a particular problem.

The results were striking.

"I was shocked," said one member of this team. "Roughly half of my student chose to do it *his* way."

"It was about the same for me," said the other. "And the whole time all I could think was that I've been teaching this course for twelve years now, and for years, nearly half of my students were solving these problems in a suboptimal way."

When I think of choice in strategy, I cannot help but think of these two and how much this experience changed their perspectives. And don't misunderstand me, I share this story not as an indictment against these terrific educators. They're great. But it highlights a reality that, if we are honest with ourselves, we all know to be true. If given a choice, most educators opt to teach their students to use the methods that they themselves prefer. I say that without passing judgment. And my hope is that, now knowing that we can do better, we might consider teaching our students a variety of learning strategies whenever possible moving forward.

The work is too important to not at least try.

The right strategy can be the difference between success and failure or between good and great. It can completely unlock learning, like it did for my daughter's reading skills. And maybe most importantly, our efforts here foster a growth mindset by giving learners permission to abandon what's not working for them in the pursuit of something better.

This conversation about learner choice will be different from the ones in prior chapters because here we are no longer teaching students to select a tangible thing like a book or a video. This choice is about selecting a course of action.

EXAMPLES OF WHERE LEARNER CHOICE IN LEARNING STRATEGY IS POSSIBLE

Because there are a lot of learner actions that can occur, let's break those down into two subcategories: processing strategies and approach strategies.

Processing strategies are the actions by the student that improve retention when they receive instruction. Terms like *engagement strategies* or *checks-for-understanding* might be more familiar to you, and if so, we are generally thinking about the same thing.

Some examples of processing strategies inlcude.

- Note-taking
- Annotations
- Think-Pair-Share
- Peer-to-peer discussion
- Questioning techniques
- Forms or games as comprehension checks
- The potential list here is extensive.

There are (at least) two ways to look at this list through the lens of learner choice. The first is to think about the potential choices available within each specific strategy. For example, remember the variety of choice-in-annotation methods we explored in chapter three? Teaching learners to discover the best method for them to employ when annotating or taking notes is its own form of learner choice.

Alternatively, acknowledging that some students are verbal processors while others may need to process by writing things down can lead to personalized practices that look to uncover which strategy or set of strategies plays to the learner's SPIN. The personalized practices here could resemble the approach we discussed for choice in instructional delivery modalities.

Having said that, let's pivot now to our second subcategory of learner actions, approach strategies, and focus our efforts on a deeper understanding of this notably different challenge. Approach strategies are the unique actions taken by the learner as they go about demonstrating their learning.

For example, let's say that all students are expected to solve the same math problem or to complete the same project. In either case, the teacher has a relatively uniform expectation for what the end result will be, but the steps the student takes along the way to arrive there may be unique to them.

It's that uniformity in the end result that sets this choice apart from the choice-in-product option we will discuss in the next chapter. Product choice is an opportunity for students to develop their own way of expressing their learning, where here, the variance is in how a task gets completed.

DEVELOPING PERSONALIZED PRACTICES FOR LEARNER CHOICE IN APPROACH STRATEGY

Again, this choice is different from those we've discussed so far, and that means our design process will differ here as well.

To begin with, the teacher will need to identify where this type of choice may be possible. Look to any assessment that has multiple steps involved. If there is some flexibility in how those steps are carried out, you've found your opportunity.

For the sake of conversation, let's say that the students have been asked to develop an infographic. The goal then is to help them design and own the steps in their approach to completing it.

As good practice, let's assume the students have received a rubric (or helped to co-create a rubric) that communicates what this infographic should accomplish, in both its content and quality. Having set clear expectations, it's time for students to get to work.

It's at this point that you will be tempted to act in a way that is in direct opposition to what we are trying to achieve here. I see it all the time. With the best of intentions for supporting students as they take on a multistep process, teachers design a lockstep approach for learners that is so specific that . . . there's no way anyone could mess it up!

Then when a student whose natural inclination would be to approach this process a different way gets lost while navigating the teacher's process, the exacerbated teacher begins to question their career choice.

In these instances, things most often go wrong for the learner for one of two reasons. Some get so bored by the monotony of this mindless measure of compliance that they space out on the details. Others simply listen too closely to their own creative inclinations, taking liberties unaccounted for by this teacher-created system. Either way, our aim will be to do the opposite of this.

Instead, look to lead learners in a way that empowers them to design their own approach. Open up the work time with a whole-class discussion that makes learners aware of the steps before them. No matter what product you are trying to produce, it's imperative that the learners be the ones who share out the potential options. At first, this can be done collectively and with the teacher guiding that conversation. But over time and with additional practice, the onus for acknowledging the steps should fall more and more on the individual student.

For example, if the aim is to construct an infographic, the teacher could simply ask the students to write out a list of all the things they think they will need to do. That list might look something like this.

- Select a program in which to build the image.
- Select a color scheme.
- Select a font family.
- Collect the required statistical information.
- Collect the required quotes or testimonials.
- Pair the content with relevant icons.
- Arrange the information visually on the page.
- Select and embed any visuals, such as images or video content.
- Download and print or share the infographic with the teacher.
- And I'm sure there are others.

Having created this list, ask students to arrange these steps individually, in the order they intend to complete them. There will need to be more whole-class conversations here, and again, encourage the learners to be the ones offering their justifications for their sequencing. Some steps will follow a logical order of operations, while others can be solely based on the learner's preference. For example, I personally like to create the general look of the infographic, like the border and the title, before I delve into finding the information, whereas others might not start their design process until their research is finished.

The final step of the personalized practice here would be to ask the learners to set a goal for how many steps they intend to finish by, we'll say, the end of the next class period. That act would be the transition into work time, as the students would individually write out their intended completion date next to each of the steps on their list.

Two class periods later, begin the class with students sharing aloud which steps they finished and what they did and learned along the way. Do your best to pose questions and pry for details. It's important to point out the variance in each learner's approach. It's also fun, as the teacher, to learn how your students work and think in their own unique ways. It gives you insights that make you a better teacher.

When a number of ideas have been shared, have students set another short-term goal and repeat this process, and continue to do that until the infographic project is complete.

Having navigated this personalized practice, the learners will be better at taking a larger task and breaking it down into its component parts. They will have learned the need to prioritize and sequence tasks, and to set microgoals to manage their own accountability. Finally, the periodic check-ins model the need for ongoing reflection, while also promoting alternative ways of approaching a given step. Clearly, there is a great deal of learner agency fostered through personalized practices that support learner choice in approach strategies.

MAKING A CHOICE IN APPROACH STRATEGY FROM A STUDENT'S PERSPECTIVE

This example was inspired by Sherry Parrish's book, Number Talks. *Parrish's emphasis on whole-class discussions to drive alternative ways of thinking perfectly aligns with the aims and implementation of learner choice in approach strategy.[1]*

Holly is a nine-year-old who is the new kid in school; her family just moved into the district from out of state. At her old school, Holly's least favorite subject, by far, was math. The teachers there had focused on the rote memorization of times tables and facts, and Holly just could not commit to memory the ninety-plus pieces of information she needed to master multiplication.

On her first day at her new school, Holly was settling in and generally enjoying herself until her teacher announced, "When you're finished, grab your math book and math notebook."

Holly's stomach sank.

As she gathered her things to transition to their math time, the teacher wrote the following problem on the board: *16x5=?*

This sent Holly into a panic.

I haven't even memorized up to twelve times twelve yet! How am I supposed to do a problem with sixteen in it, she wondered.

The teacher had asked the class to independently (and quietly) solve the problem. Holly hadn't memorized sixteen times five, so she worked through the problem the only way she knew how.

Holly thought, Okay, five times six is thirty. Drop down the zero and carry the three . . .

It wasn't long before the teacher asked the students to take turns sharing their answers aloud. Holly was not about to do that, even though she felt pretty good about her answer.

---

1 Sherry Parrish, *Number Talks: Whole Number Computation* (Sausalito, CA: Math Solutions, 2014).

As the students shared, the teacher recorded each response on the board without affirming or correcting any answer that was given.

When all the various answers had been recorded, the teacher called on Holly's friend, Jaydn, and asked, "Jaydn, you said that sixteen times five is eighty. How did you arrive at that answer?"

"Well," Jadyn began, "I broke down the sixteen into ten and six because I know that five times ten is fifty and five times six is thirty. Then I just put fifty and thirty together and got eighty."

Jaydn's approach seemed so simple, and yet was so foreign to Holly, that had she not gotten the same answer herself, she would have really doubted that it could be correct.

The teacher just nodded her head while saying, "Hmm, that's interesting," before asking, "Did anyone else get eighty as their answer using a different strategy?"

Enola raised her hand, and the teacher called on her.

"Okay," Enola began, "I got what Jaydn got but I took the five and doubled it to get ten. Then I took half of sixteen, which is eight. I timesed those two, the eight and the ten, and got eighty."

Again, "Interesting" was all the teacher uttered before calling on another student who also wanted to share.

"I got eighty, too," said Adam, "but how I did it was I know that twenty times five is one hundred, and that sixteen is four less than twenty. So I timesed four by five, which is twenty, and then I subtracted it from one hundred and got eighty."

Jaydn's comments alone had left Holly stunned, but collectively, the first ten minutes of math class had blown Holly's mind. She had never realized that there were so many ways to solve a multiplication problem!

When it came time to practice, Holly found herself using Jaydn's method, at least most of the time. But there were also times when Adam's idea of overshooting the number and then subtracting back to it really came in handy.

This was just the beginning of Holly learning to personalize her own approach to math.

CHAPTER 8

LEARNER CHOICE IN PRODUCT (ASSESSMENT)

At the front of my classroom, there's a sign that reads, "Life isn't about finding yourself. Life is about creating yourself." I posted this quote from George Bernard Shaw in my room with the hope that it would be a constant reminder to everyone that to create is to be fully human. We are all creators, and chiefly, of ourselves.

Holding that belief, I'm always so disheartened when I hear someone say, "I'm just not creative." That's such a self-defeating lie. It's fundamentally untrue. It goes against our very nature. But I do recognize that creativity is like a muscle; it needs to be flexed often. It's like Maya Angelou once said about creativity, "The more you use, the more you have."

Part of our job as learning-experience designers is to creatively construct scenarios that ask students to flex their own creative muscle. Personalized practices for learner choice in product is an ideal place to do just that.

The *product* in a learning experience is the learner's representation of their knowledge, understanding, or mastery of a concept or skill. If that seems a little vague, it might be easier to think of the product as the thing that gets graded.

For the sake of clarity, here are several examples of what we will identify as a product.

- A presentation
- A speech
- An essay
- A test
- A Socratic discussion
- An infographic
- A poster
- A PSA
- A performance
- A skit
- A commercial
- And infinitely more

In the last chapter, we pointed out that there are a number of ways a student might personalize their approach to developing a singular product. In this chapter, we will explore what it looks like to offer learners their choice in the type of product itself. That means the student will be free to choose how they show what they know.

Before we go any further, there's something we need to be clear about. Choice boards.

Some people call them choice charts, others prefer learning menus, but no matter the name, the practice is generally the same. Students are given a list of potential assignments and are asked to complete a set number of the options offered on the choice board.

Are choice boards engaging? Sure. Are choice boards a great break from the single-assignment approach to assessment? Absolutely. Generally, I like choice boards. But giving a student a choice board does not mean the learning is personalized.

Wait . . . what? Why not?

Well, for starters, the teacher is the one creating the options. Being able to develop the idea *itself* is the creativity flex that we want to simulate here. That's the mental heavy lifting that choice boards so often remove entirely from the equation.

You may be thinking, "Well, not the way I do it. I add in an open-ended option so that if a student has an idea, they can pursue it."

While I like that opportunity within the choice-board strategy, leaving that door open does not mean the learning is personalized. In practice, the only students who take on that open-ended option are those who already have the self-efficacy and the creative muscle to step into that space. The vast majority of the students will still opt to punt on the mental responsibility of having to conceptualize their own idea. They'll just use what the teacher provides because that's easier.

With or without choice boards, when students are given a choice-in-product decision, it can be disheartening when they elect to pursue the most obvious and expedient option. As practitioners, our response to that disposition shouldn't be to stop offering this choice. However, we will need to keep this learner perspective in mind as we design.

There is tremendous potential for learner growth here. This is a chance to promote innovative thinking by asking learners to merge the things they are passionate about with their coursework. It's a moment when they can showcase their best skills (strengths) and foster new ones in the development of something they care about (interest).

In a world where technology is relentless in its takeover of the routinized tasks of our day, the future belongs to the creative. And our kids are counting on us to help. Let's look to design experiences that prepare them to own the responsibility of conceptualizing and creating a product that plays to their SPIN and is representative of their learning.

DEVELOPING PERSONALIZED PRACTICES
FOR LEARNER CHOICE IN PRODUCT

Teaching someone to be more creative is no simple task. There are some students, even very bright ones, who quickly shut down at the mere mention of the word *creativity*.

It's imperative that we begin by clearly conveying the *why* behind this personalized practice. Feel free to use some of the points made in this chapter, along with your own, to help you advocate for why furthering one's own creative capacity is important. And don't overlook that this choice will ask students to be vulnerable. Acknowledge that up front. Reassure them that there is a plan and a process in place to support them. Stress that you, and their classmates, are there to help.

The rest of this chapter will look a little different from the others. Instead of providing an example and a story, we will explore several tips and some personalized practices that give implementation ideas for how to foster creativity. Again, it is up to you, the designer of this experience, to learn and then commit to using one or a combination of these ideas, remixing them or making new ones up on your own that give your students the chance to develop as creators.

FOSTERING CREATIVITY TIP #1:
TEACH CREATORS HOW TO IDENTIFY THE GOAL

When students are given an assignment that affords them the chance to create, too often they fixate on the product itself instead of seeing that product as a platform through which they can show what they know. The best illustration of this is when students produce a video for class that has ninety seconds of actual content, followed by a twelve-minute blooper reel.

Teach the students to see this product as an expression of what they have learned. Their aim should be to showcase that learning in full, which means they will need a clear understanding of all they should try to capture or demonstrate.

One of my favorite personalized practices to help with this is to have the whole class collaborate on writing the rubric for this assignment.

Rubrics for choice-in-product assignments can be tricky, which is why talking openly about what should be included in each product is important. Prepare for this conversation by building a rubric on your own that captures your expectations. This will prep you to be the subtle hand that guides the dialogue, ensuring that the essential components are present. However, stay open. Expect to tweak a few things as a result of the students' input.

In class, hand each student a blank rubric (or give them the option of using a digital copy as a processing choice). Filling this out during the discussion will help with engagement and make the details stick. An example template of this resource can be downloaded on my website at AndrewDEaston.com.

Now you're ready to chat.

Begin by asking students to reflect on their learning and share what they believe they should have taken away from it. Have them keep a list of the key pieces of information and skills. Identify these pieces as nonnegotiables that, regardless of what they choose as their product, need to be expressed in what they create.

As you discuss things, don't be afraid to zoom out and speak on a metacognitive level. For example, stress that this type of conversation, whether you have it with others or by yourself, is an essential step of the creative process. Clarity about the ultimate goal is what gives a product meaning. Also, note that writing their own rubric is a big deal in their development as mature learners with true agency. As the session comes to a close, ask them to reflect on how much more confident they are in their approach having had this conversation.

If you're worried that you don't have the thirty minutes it takes to facilitate this personalized practice, don't be. Just do it. Any work time lost to hold this discussion will be made up later through the level of clarity the learners will have about what is being asked of them. Let's not overlook that this will also lead to a better end product.

One last thing to anticipate is the need to address the question, How much does the quality of the product itself matter? This is a hotly contested point on creativity rubrics. Some educators contend that the content should be all that matters, but something just doesn't feel right about a student earning an A- for scribbling some stick figures and text onto a half-torn sheet of notebook paper. Others will adamantly defend that the quality of the product should matter, but that has its shortcomings, too.

Ultimately, if our aim here is to push students to flex their creativity, quality needs to be a factor, even if that means the product is "scored," even if that's not in a way that contributes to the final grade that goes into the grade book. Talk this point out as a part of the whole-class co-creation of the rubric itself.

And while you are advocating for the learners to add a *Quality* column to the rubric, go ahead and promote the idea of phrasing it as *Quality+Risk* Why add *Risk*? Well, adding *Risk* to the rubric communicates a truth about innovation—it often requires a leap of faith—and the last thing we want to do is punish a student whose jump falls flat. This is a powerful point to make to learners, that there is a relationship between these two. Now, ideally, every creative endeavor would produce a high-quality, high-risk product, but creativity does not always manifest itself that way. Great successes are so often the result of trial and error, of learning through iteration. Therefore, consider scoring the Quality+Risk column this way: the greater the risk, the less the quality should matter, and the lower the risk, the more the quality should come into play. This offers a nice balance that simultaneously promotes creative ambition while deterring students from opting for the easiest approach imaginable.

To recap: discuss the essentials that demonstrate that the key concepts and skills have been learned. Address the issue of product quality, and consider adding risk to the conversation and rubric as well. From there, ask learners to reference their Learner-Interest Inventory (or give a quick survey) to help them identify some strengths, preferences, and interests that they might use to their advantage with this creative effort. This step can be facilitated in a way similar to the choice-in-topic example from chapter five. Then, prior to creating, have students self-assess the degree of risk they are taking, and ask them to do this again for quality and risk after their product has been developed to completion. These steps will ensure clear content expectations and authentic creative efforts from the learners.

FOSTERING CREATIVITY TIP #2: TEACH CREATORS TO KNOW AND USE THEIR INTERESTS AND STRENGTHS

Another struggle with asking students to be creative is that they can have a very difficult time with not seeing everything that they do for school as an *assignment*. From the student's perspective, assignments are prescriptive, they are busy work, and they are to be completed according to someone else's expectations.

Hmm, I wonder why that is? But I digress . . .

In contrast, consider how we might position the student to learn, from experience, that a job well done can be far more satisfying than any mark you receive from your teacher. Can we restore the learner's faith that joy and fulfillment can be found in learning, if only we pour a piece of who we are into what we do? I believe we can, and that's the aim here.

To do this, we need personalized practices that point out a student's strengths (among which are skills), preferences, and interests. Then we need to do the work of teaching them how to incorporate the best parts of who they are into how and what they create.

What better place is there to find a learner's strengths than the Learner-Interest Inventory? A personalized practice for learner choice in product would be to direct students to that document and have them retrieve any information pertaining to their personal interests, talents, and technical skills. Have them extract that info, jot it down, and then entertain how each might be leveraged in creating a product for this assignment. Set the expectation that students do this for multiple strengths and skills, not just the obvious one.

Most students will struggle with this at first, so hold a whole-class conversation that models the type of thinking that applies these pieces to an academic setting. Call on students, ask them to share a strength or skill, then ask them to hypothetically apply that trait to the assignment at hand. As you lead this conversation, stress that learners focus on merging the attributes with the coursework, instead of being overly concerned about the medium through which it will be captured.

For example, I once had a student who traveled on the weekends doing competitive dance. When she was asked where her interests and academic work might meet, she considered expressing her learning through interpretive dance.

At first, I was a little skeptical, but I said, "Yeah, why not. But how will you make sure that an audience, untrained in reading interpretive dance, will be able to pick up on your message?"

She ultimately decided to film her performance and to add captions throughout the video that relayed the information, quotes, and level of understanding the product needed to convey. It was really well done, and afterward, she talked proudly about the time, effort, and creative energy she had poured into this piece because it meant something to her.

Another choice-in-product exercise that simulates this type of thinking was first shared with me by education author and speaker Mandy Froehlich. In this personalized practice, the goal is to teach learners to be strategic when selecting a product to convey their understanding.

Here's how it works.

The teacher assigns three prompts and tells the learners that they have three different ways of showing what they know for each. Let's say we've selected an essay, a speech, and an infographic. Each product choice can only be used once, so the question is, How will you choose which product to pair with each prompt?

Do you amplify one effort by pairing a product strength with a topic you know a lot about, even if that means pairing two weaknesses in another effort? Or will you leverage your greatest product strength to compensate for a topic you may not know quite as well? Maybe the decision is driven by the content instead of the medium?

I prefer this practice as formative work and would introduce it along with a whole-class conversation that explores the myriad of decisions the learner can potentially make here. I love the metacognitive merit of this activity as a personalized practice that better equips learners to make academically intentional decisions when given a choice-in-product opportunity.

FOSTERING CREATIVITY TIP #3: TEACH LEARNERS HOW TO PUSH THEMSELVES CREATIVELY

When working out, it's healthiest to build your muscles using a variety of exercises, and the same is true for creativity. Creativity grows not just through opportunity but, more specifically, through things like iteration, exposure to new ideas, limitations, and the acquisition of new tools. For tip number three, we will explore an example of each, as a way to add more breadth and depth to how educators might think about designing personalized practices to foster learner agency when it comes to choice-in-product opportunities.

Iteration

Every teacher recognizes the value of iteration. It's how we grow in this profession. Yet, when it comes to our students' creative opportunities, we tend to limit that type of learning to one specific instance within a semester or year. It's accounted for in "The _____ Project" that always takes place during the month of _____. And while it's great that the students get this chance to be creative, does this one-and-done experience allow learners to fail forward in their creative endeavors?

Probably not.

To be fair, one of the primary factors that prevents teachers from building in more of these types of choice-in-product opportunities is *time*. Projects take weeks, not days, and there are other content and skills that must be covered.

If this sounds familiar, I would challenge you to consider designing at least one short, low-stakes formative project per unit that offers learners some creative agency. And if you're too pressed for time, consider designing a choice-in-product challenge with a time limit. Cooking shows are notorious for using this tactic: the contestants are given a handful of materials or an objective and are then asked to produce a quality and creative dish in less than thirty minutes. Educators can implement similar practices to give students exposure to a variety of creative experiences. Maybe the first twenty-minute challenge asks that students capture the day's learning in an artistic image. The next time, they might be asked to do so in a short video. A third challenge might offer them the complete freedom to choose what they create. With each round comes the chance for learners to develop new skills, to practice conveying their understanding using alternative methods, and—maybe most importantly—to feel pushed by their coursework in ways beyond rigor.

Through these personalized practices, learners are growing in their creative capacity for self-efficacy so that when it comes time for the big annual project (that major moment of choice), they have the experiences and the confidence to come up with an idea and deliver on it.

Exposure to New Ideas

Innovation often occurs when an idea from one context is applied to another scenario by someone with a different skill set and experiences.

As such, the more that educators can expose learners to different methods for demonstrating learning, the greater the variance they are likely to see in the products created. For this reason, iteration and exposure to new ideas should go hand in hand as a personalized practice.

For example, let's say that students just finished their first twenty-minute choice-in-product challenge. As that time frame comes to an end, there are likely several examples of student work that could be championed to the group. As the teacher, look for and highlight aloud any examples of creative projects that really captured the academic content well. Point out and praise unique demonstrations of learning, regardless of their quality. And brag on and build up the students who managed to do quality work under the time constraints. Not only will this improve the class culture through student recognition and recognition of noteworthy efforts, but those pieces will stick with students as examples and stretch their perception of what is possible in the future.

Limitations

If you really want to have some fun when designing personalized practices for choice in product, start developing creative opportunities that come with constraints.

No, that's not an oxymoron. Adding parameters to your personalized practices can push students to embrace limitations rather than complain about them. These could be specific constraints, like the time frames idea shared earlier, or students could be given a limited number of materials to work with that either must be incorporated into the end product or are the only materials they can use in creating the end product. This concept can go past materials to words or topics. Imagine asking students to help you create a list of ten random words, and then you can flip that list on them by asking the students to create something that captures their learning from the day that also includes any seven of those ten words.

Limitations can also help move students off stale ideas, like the perpetual creation of slide decks, by saying something like, "You can create whatever you want as long as it's a product you have not created for an assignment in this class before."

Given that most creative endeavors in life are carried out inside the proverbial box and with limited resources, simulating this type of creative effort is tremendous practice for cultivating a learner's ability to be innovative.

Acquisition of a New Tool

In an ideal world, the task would always drive the selection of the tool used to achieve it. That's the modern EdTech mantra in education circles. But if we are honest with ourselves, there are times when we are presented with a new tech tool, and almost instantly we see the potential it has to transform how we approach our work.

What's odd is that despite how tech-savvy the younger generation always seems to be, most students are surprisingly limited in their knowledge of tech tools for creativity.

Recognizing this, a personalized practice worth considering is teaching learners about the latest tech tools they might use for being creative. A great way to do this is simply to put together a list of tools and then link each to a YouTube video that explains how to use it.

If that sounds like a great idea, but you're not sure where to begin, my website AndrewDEaston.com has an example that you can use.

There is just something beautiful about the learning that is exhibited during a choice-in-product experience. It has tremendous depth, it makes connections with prior learning and passions, and it produces a piece that is fully academic but touched by the creative soul of the student. As learning-experience designers, we must create both the opportunities for learners to grow in these ways and the strategies necessary to foster creativity as a skill in the students we serve.

CHAPTER 9

LEARNER CHOICE IN PACE

At one time, it was extremely difficult to convince teachers to try and offer this choice because many educators could not imagine what their role in the learning process might look like if they weren't the ones driving it.

But then, the various learning scenarios during the COVID-19 pandemic changed all of that.

In just a few short months, the education community worldwide was forced into facilitating learning remotely, and our collective capacity to lead asynchronous learning reached an all-time high.

During that time, a lot of things changed. Internet connectivity was expanded. Districts scrambled to get a device in the hands of every student. The learning management systems that had previously been used as little more than the digital equivalent of a *Past Assignments* folder were transformed into a place where each component part of a unit plan could be housed within a learning module. Educators became Zoom experts and many began producing their own instructional video content.

And that's just on the tech side of things.

The pandemic learning experience also exposed two truths about asynchronous learning that we will explore in detail in this chapter. (1) Clear communication with learners (and their families) on how to navigate an asynchronous, choice-in-pace experience is critical. (2) Most students lack the soft skills necessary to stay organized and keep themselves accountable if the teacher (or a family member) is not there to watch over them. Because of this reality, striving for *teacher clarity* and *learner agency* was at the forefront of the pedagogical best practices at the time.

However, conversations about asynchronous learning long preceded the pandemic, when we were just discussing *learner pace*. Making that connection is important because it may be helpful to think about learner choice as asynchronous learning in an in-person setting. In this chapter, we will explore how to empower learners with the freedom to move asynchronously through one or several learning experiences (think modules) according to their own sequencing and ideal learning time frame.

Of course, there are a number of things to think about with that.

AN EXAMPLE OF THE PREP WORK FOR LEADING CHOICE-IN-PACE LEARNING

STEP #1: DETERMINE THE SCOPE AND TIME FRAME. Just how long and for how many lessons will the learner have the responsibility of pacing the experience? As for the time duration, personalized practices might include the chance for learners to determine the pace for one day's learning, then two days, then a week, etc. This scaffolding builds in a gradual transfer of responsibility that is necessary for learners as they acclimate to this new expectation.

STEP #2A: BUILD THE NECESSARY RESOURCES. Honestly, there is a lot of up-front work to be done here. If the learners are going to be able to move at their own pace, all the materials will need to be available to them on day one. That means every video, resource, assignment, and rubric. This responsibility is best accomplished as a shared effort among a teacher team. Persevere through this step, and your reward will be no lesson planning once the experience gets started. *It's totally worth it.*

STEP #2B (OPTIONAL): CONSIDER BUILDING IN LEARNER CHOICE. If you have done the initial scaffolding work with personalized practices, don't forget to add any choice opportunities the learners might be prepared to handle. This gets to something that we will explore in more detail later: layering in multiple choice opportunities.

STEP #3: ORGANIZE THE MATERIALS. Whether it's in a paper packet, a hyperdoc, a Google Site, or an LMS, be thoughtful about how you organize and sequence the materials and choices being offered to learners. If students will be presented with multiple learning modules, make sure that there is uniformity in the look, layout, and progression of those experiences. This alleviates both student and teacher angst about assignment expectations.

STEP #4A: SEEK OUT FEEDBACK AND REVISE FOR CLARITY. Whether you created this experience alone or as a team, ask a colleague, or better yet a student, to look things over to see if it all makes sense. Where there are holes in the clarity of instruction, directions, or sequencing, make revisions.

STEP #4B (OPTIONAL): CREATE ALTERNATIVE WAYS TO COMMUNICATE ASSIGNMENT DIRECTIONS. When I started offering assignment directions in both written and video form, the number of questions I had about the details of the work dropped dramatically. Another tool to leverage here would be a text-to-speech reader that would allow learners to have the directions read to them. Consider playing to your learner groups' preferences and strengths by delivering directions through multiple modalities.

STEP #5: BE THOUGHTFUL ABOUT WHAT IS OFFERED TO STUDENTS WHO FINISH EARLY. The learning opportunities being offered to students who finish early will play a significant role in defining the class culture during choice-in-pace learning. If the only reward for the diligent student is more busy work, no one will care about finishing early and the impact of that will be felt throughout the room. That being said, if the opportunity is free time or the chance to play a game, some students will rush their efforts and turn in poor quality work, just to get to the end.

Instead, consider creating learning experiences that do one or more of the following:

- Deepen the learning
- Give learners recognition
- Connect learners with an expert
- Connect learners with an authentic audience
- Connect learners with an authentic experience
- Give students a chance to be competitive
- Give students a chance to earn or collect something
- Give students a chance to create something

There is also the potential here to offer these types of options on a choice board or to take more of a choice-in-product, PBL, or CBL approach by developing their own project once they have finished early.

DEVELOPING PERSONALIZED PRACTICES FOR LEARNER CHOICE IN PACE

The previous section outlined how to amass the resources and materials needed to launch a choice-in-pace experience. Now it's time to think through how we might teach learners to better handle the responsibility of moving at their own pace. Our aim will be to help students set both immediate and long-term goals and then to develop a clear plan for how they will accomplish them.

Goal Setting

Okay, while the idea of students setting goals is no doubt familiar, it's important to point out that not all goals are set for the same type of purpose or outcome.

For example, sometimes students will set academic achievement goals and measure them in the form of grades. Sometimes skill building is the goal and is measured by demonstration. It's possible to have social goals, emotional goals, behavioral goals, or a combination of all three, and it goes without saying that a learner can be thoughtful about pursuing multiple goals simultaneously.

Here, where the desire is to teach students how to effectively manage the pace of their learning, the learners will be asked to set productivity goals that can be measured by something as simple as timely completion. The act of setting productivity goals establishes clear expectations for students. Achieving those goals builds academic momentum and confidence, which benefits the learning through an increase in time-on-task behavior.

Success breeds success.

However, don't overlook the importance of the student being the one with the ability to own the plan. The key here is to turn this into a personalized practice. That's what we will strive to teach, initially, and then teach how to stay accountable over the duration of the learning experience, which is a different matter altogether.

In the following sections, we will look at a few ideas for how to support learner productivity over a shorter choice-in-pace window of time and also during a longer time frame.

An Idea for Short-Term Choice-in-Pace Opportunities

While learning remotely during the spring of 2020, my daughter and son, who were nine and six years old at the time, were struggling to stay on top of their schoolwork (like most at-home learners during the pandemic). The learning was all asynchronous, no Zoom, and it was recommended that the list of assignments be completed by the end of each day.

It was fairly common for them to have between four and seven assignments, and my daughter's schoolwork would often have several steps or assignments within each subject area. We needed a system where the two of them could see what they needed to complete and feel themselves making progress.

To that end, I created a Kanban Board for each of them on poster paper and hung those boards on the walls of our dining room. If you are unfamiliar with Kanban Boards, the concept is simple. It's a table with two rows and three columns. Across the first row, I wrote out the title for each column: *To Do*, *Doing*, and *Done*.

Each morning, the kids and I would look up their tasks for the day and write out on Post-it Notes the various assignments they needed to complete. Each Post-it was added to the to-do column of their board. Over the course of the day, as they began an assignment, they would move the corresponding Post-it from *To Do* to *Doing*, and eventually, to *Done*.

The goal was to get four Post-its moved by lunchtime. Any extra just meant less work in the afternoon.

True to my own ideals, we created a recognition system where, for every five completed Post-its, they would receive a star that they could add to the top of their chart. Five stars earned them the treat of their choice.

When learners are in control of the pace of their learning for a relatively short time, like one to three days, a Kanban Board is a great personalized practice for teaching learners how to break down and manage that responsibility.

In the event that you don't have enough wall space around the room for each student to have their own Kanban Board and Post-its, this practice can be done digitally through a program like Trello. It's also possible to facilitate that same practice within a shared and editable Google Slides deck.

An Idea for Longer-Term Choice-in-Pace Opportunities

In 2008, for some reason I thought it would be a good idea to offer learners an eight-week window of time as my first attempt with choice-in-pace learning. Looking back on it, things honestly could have gone a lot worse, but I'll admit that I spent the majority of the time monitoring student behaviors, encouraging them to stay on task. By the last week of the quarter when everything was due, many of the students were frantically scrambling to make up for seven weeks of procrastination, which only led to them feeling frustrated as they hurriedly submitted poorly completed work.

But I learned from it, and so did my students.

The two greatest needs were obvious. The students needed a plan for how to pace themselves and a daily accountability measure. My job as their teacher was clear: help them see it and help them own it, in that order.

To try to help them see it, I created a blank unit calendar and a list of every step of every assignment they were expected to complete. Think of it as a giant to-do list. Next to each task on that list, I put a time frame for how long it might take to complete that item, generally speaking—so twenty minutes, forty minutes, etc.

Moving all those pieces to completion was the long-term goal.

In the class period before the unit began, I spent five minutes communicating the *why*. I shared that adulthood is often about managing multiple responsibilities, moving one or several pieces forward, day by day, in order to meet hard-and-fast, long-term deadlines. I acknowledged that school often teaches the opposite message. If they expect their boss to give them bite-sized, thirty-minute-or-less tasks and to then look over their shoulder the whole time while they work *and* to assume full responsibility should they fail—well, they're dreaming.

It was always great to challenge learners to step up and step into a level of responsibility that they often claimed they were ready for but rarely had the tools or the skills to own. After my little speech, I handed out the calendars and asked each of them to copy every item from the to-do list onto the calendar when and where it made sense. In this moment, the students were doing the teacher's work of creating the curriculum calendar for the unit.

Once everyone finished mapping out the next seven weeks, I asked a rhetorical question: "So how many of you fully expect the next seven weeks to go precisely according to this plan?" Most knew me well enough to smirk instead of answer.

We then discussed strategies for how to get caught up. I pointed out the blank homework space at the bottom of the calendar and said that they would only take home the homework that they gave themselves, but that once they got behind, they were expected to use homework as a way to keep up with their pace.

This took care of the pacing guide. Now we needed that daily accountability piece.

When I started this work, I would make my way around the room each day asking students what they hoped to accomplish. Over time, I began to work smarter and created a hard-copy handout that asked learners to write out what they intended to accomplish by the end of class. The expectation was that they communicate this as a SMART goal—well, okay, maybe it was more of an SM goal. My only real expectations were that they be written as a complete sentence and be measurable.

At the start of class each day, every student's bell work activity was to record their daily goal on the handout. I would circulate throughout the room, greeting students as they entered and checking daily goals to make sure they fit my two criteria. If one didn't, the student and I would chat about it and revise it then and there.

When there was roughly five minutes left in class, I would ask the students to stop working and reflect on what they had accomplished that day. Beneath the daily goal on the handout was a space that prompted students with "Did you meet your goal? Circle Yes or No." If the answer was no, they were expected to explain why they didn't meet it and then modify their unit calendar, give themselves homework, or both to adjust their pacing guide.

The answers that came with the *why not* were unfailingly honest: "I talked too much." "I was tired." "I spent too much time playing on my phone." "I gave myself too much to do for the time I had."

Now, if we are being honest, what adult hasn't experienced the same things, right?!

It's reassuring to learners to acknowledge that these types of things happen to adults as well. The important thing is for them to recognize it and make adjustments. It's interesting to watch students start to police themselves once they see that something is routinely squashing their own productivity. This process is truly one of the most transformative toward fostering learner agency.

Who knew that students could learn to take responsibility for the pace of their learning in the time it takes to do bell work and an exit ticket each day? If you're interested in downloading the pacing handout I use, you can find it at AndrewDEaston.com.

Just like they do with the other choices, students simply need a little guidance up front, the opportunity to try things on their own, and your support when they need to fail forward. The examples shared here are just that, examples. It's up to you to create your own. Just keep in mind that it's so rewarding for students to set goals and to achieve them, and when it comes to choice in pace, no matter how you support the learners, be sure that they have a plan for what to do and maybe even how to revise it.

CHAPTER 10

LEARNER CHOICE IN COMMUNICATION

For many students, talking with their teachers feels somewhere between slightly awkward at best and downright terrifying at its worst, at least initially.

There's a myriad of reasons for this. Some learners carry a real fear of sounding unintelligent. Others don't like the feeling of vulnerability that comes with admitting they're confused or need help. There's also a fairly large number of students who try to come across as if they don't care at all about their schoolwork. Sure, some of that is social posturing, but more often than not, it has more to do with the fear of failure and them running away from any expectations that they may not be able to meet.

The point here is this: it's challenging to get students to communicate about their learning, and a lot of that has to do with a lack of self-confidence. If the goal of personalization is to foster learner agency, then we will need to do more than just teach students how to walk the walk; they need to be able to talk the talk, too.

Take a moment and ask yourself how many of your students you see as being effective advocates for their own academic needs? If that number isn't 100 percent, then we still have some work to do to empower every voice.

In education today, there is a clear need for strategies that intentionally open the lines of communication between learners and their teachers during the learning process. To do this well will take more than just getting them literally to speak. The personalized practices throughout this book teach learners how to think deeply about their learning, and in this chapter, we will explore ways to promote academic dialogue and foster a class culture where it's okay to talk and ask questions.

To accomplish this, it helps if we teach students to recognize the specific type of question or support they need. We will discuss how to do this in the "Knowing When to Reach Out" section that follows. After that, we'll explore ways to offer learners their choice in communication modality during the "Knowing How to Reach Out" segment. The chapter will end on the topic of "Teacher Feedback," where we will consider how our response to our learners reaching out can create a more communicative class culture as a whole.

KNOWING WHEN TO REACH OUT

The first step is to disarm the misnomer that there is such a thing as a stupid question. To do this, we'll start in a familiar place: leading learners through the *why*.

Take ten minutes to teach your class just how important communication is in the process of learning. This point may feel obvious, but it's likely not something that has been explicitly expressed to them before. To fully seize this moment, go beyond talking generally about the role of communication and express, in a public way, just how much this matters to you as their teacher. Share your heart for how much you care and want to see them grow in their ability to advocate for themselves.

Segue into an acknowledgment that asking a question can be uncomfortable, but explain that we all have questions at times. Stress that asking questions is an essential part of learning and not an indictment on a person's intelligence.

At this point, launch into teaching the learners the differences between *a quick question, a learning question,* and *feedback.* These terms are loose; use whatever language you wish here, but the point is that if we can give a name and a categorization to different types of responses, then students won't feel as self-conscious about asking.

Quick questions are just that, simple and brief. Most often they are answered with a short, knowledge-level response. When is this due? or, What do we do next? would be examples of quick questions. In this case, the learner is just missing a detail that they need to press on.

Learning questions are slightly more complex questions that are asked in the midst of the learning process. While some may only require a brief response, it's more common for learning questions to take a longer time to answer. That's because there is often some teaching or reteaching that needs to occur. "When I did this, I got this answer, and it's wrong, but I don't understand why?" would be one example of a learning question. "I just don't understand this. Can you help me?" is another example of the student reaching out while they learn.

Feedback is the third type, and it's easy to spot because students ask for this type of communication after having made an attempt at demonstrating their understanding. Just hearing the term, *feedback,* will no doubt bring to mind student questions like "Can you check this for me?" or "Am I doing this right?"

It's important to point out that when learner choice is available, *feedback* may look more like the student asking for permission, requesting additional materials, or wanting to create their own options. I'm always thrilled when I hear, "Mr. Easton, is it okay if I . . . ?" because that's the sound of the learner assuming ownership over the opportunity the choice is providing. Another great example is "You know what would be helpful . . . " followed by a suggestion. Listen for these types of learner feedback, as they signal that the personalized practices are working.

Consider posting these question types prominently on the wall of your classroom as a constant point of reference.

Help reinforce this new terminology by asking learners to recall it in real time. When a student raises their hand, as you approach them ask, "Is this a quick question, a learning question, or are you seeking feedback?"

At first, they will need to pause and consider it, but before long, learners will incorporate this language into their sentence starters. For example, "Mr. Easton, can you help me with a learning question . . . ?" Naming the question takes a great deal of the fear out of asking it because students can see the purpose behind it.

KNOWING HOW TO REACH OUT

I know I'm nerdy, but I find it fascinating just how much the modality of expression impacts the depth and breadth of a student's response. For example, an extrovert who is a verbal processor might need a three-to-five-minute conversation to pose a question and talk through it, but if they were asked to write it out, it might only be one sentence long. Similarly, a shy introvert may never willingly speak aloud but could pour out their thoughts at length onto a page.

With that reality in mind, there's the potential here for personalized practices to help learners uncover the best way for them to communicate with their teacher. This is the learner choice-in-communication conversation, and it's a matter of finding the right modality.

The personalized practices here are similar to those we've discussed before. Learners simply need the systematized scaffolding experience of practicing with various modalities to determine which avenue(s) are most effective for them. This applies both to asking questions and also to receiving feedback and support, which we will discuss later in this chapter.

Here's an example. In a longer, choice-in-pace experience, I always add a place on the daily goals handout for students to write down any questions they have for me. I also verbally probe for questions as I circulate around the room. And I like to require students to record a week-in-review recap video, where students reflect on their learning using Flipgrid.

The aim here is to make enough avenues available that each learner will inevitably find the one or two modes through which they are the most expressive. That's the personalized piece. But I still make all three available and—at times—required, because I want to push the learners to become better at communicating across a variety of modalities, playing both to their strengths and their needs.

TEACHER FEEDBACK

It's true that what you say matters, but what a teacher does also speaks volumes. In this section, we will highlight a few recommended actions that will help to foster a more communicative class culture.

- **REFER TO STUDENTS BY NAME.** At least once a class period, show each student that you know who they are by addressing them by their first name.
- **PROVE YOU ARE LISTENING BY PARAPHRASING.** While I'm not a big fan of the cheesy phrases like "What I'm hearing you say is . . . ," I do believe that good communicators build rapport by paraphrasing the points or questions of others.
- **PUBLICLY PRAISE THE BEHAVIORS YOU WANT TO PROMOTE.** For example, if a student asks if they can create their own option, consider asking for everyone's attention for a moment to share what was asked and to praise that kind of thinking. Try not to embarrass the student, of course.
- **DON'T GET TOO COMFY.** In a learner choice-in-pace learning experience, there is the temptation to take a seat at the front during moments when there doesn't appear to be any student questions. Don't sit. Be diligent about actively moving throughout the room because there are some questions that students won't ask unless you're accessible and it's convenient to engage you.

- **DRAW ATTENTION TO THE REVISIONS YOU MAKE AS A RESULT OF LEARNER FEEDBACK.** If a conversation with a student leads you to make a noteworthy change in the lesson, materials, or options, thank that student in front of the class and point out the revision. This reinforces that you are a listener and that learner input can create change.
- **GIVE LEARNERS AN OPPORTUNITY TO USE THE FEEDBACK YOU GIVE THEM.** Teach learners the value of receiving feedback by providing them with an opportunity to use it. Consider allowing students to improve their grade if they rewrite, retake, redo, or revise their work. Alternatively, maybe the feedback from one assignment is used to establish a growth goal for a similar assessment in the future. Find ways to teach learners how and why feedback matters.
- **OFFER FEEDBACK THROUGH THE LEARNER'S PREFERRED MODALITY.** We all have experienced the gut punch that is watching students crumple up and throw away unread feedback that you spent hours upon hours scribbling in the margins of their work. If students aren't reading your written feedback, maybe it's time to use a different modality. Beyond the traditional written form, you could type in a digital document, use an add-on like Mote to leave audio snippets on a digital document, or capture your feedback in a short video. Through personalized practices, find out which mode each learner is most likely to listen to and start pouring your feedback out in that space. It may even save you time!

If we are going to teach our learners how to be thoughtful in their approach to learning, we need to be a sounding board for them as they grow. Yet, we cannot provide this timely support if the lines of communication are not open and clear. That's why it's our job to think deeply and act intentionally about what we can do to tear down the walls that students build up and use those same bricks to build bridges.

CHAPTER 11

LEARNER CHOICE IN LEARNING SPACE

To conclude these middle chapters on learner choice, we will explore the topic of choice in learning space. This is a conversation that is largely about seating options, seating arrangements, and learning stations. However, the classroom environment as a whole and the learner's experience within it should be a part of any learning-space discussion.

In this chapter, we will look at learning space through the lens of learner choice. Expect to take your thinking one step deeper, past chair preference, to a place where the learning-space design complements the task at hand and empowers learners with the responsibility to create their own optimal learning conditions.

As is the case with all learner choices, the personalized practices come first. Teach learners how to make academically motivated modifications to their environment before they are granted the freedom to choose. When scaffolded well, this approach to learning space extends the learner's metacognitive efforts and, as a result, boosts their self-efficacy and productivity. Those benefits ultimately enhance the learning.

Wait, I thought this was going to be a conversation about flex seating?!

Eh . . . kinda. But, not exactly.

In education, learning-space design has become what the tech-tool craze of the early 2000s used to be. There's a certain fascination with *the shiny new object* and not enough attention being paid to the purpose for which it is being implemented and consistently used.

Don't get me wrong, I like the optics of flex seating. Those spaces always feel much more free, fresh, and fun. But the learning is not personalized by simply compiling enough high tops, low tops, beanbag chairs, and carpet squares to offer students their pick of where to sit.

Instead, let's strive to teach learners how to take ownership of their ability to stay on task and accomplish their goals. Let that be the *why*. With that goal, yes, there will be times when our personalized practices promote being seated where the students are most comfortable, but they can also address things like group dynamics, the use of electronics, and seeking out other students and resources that support the work in front of you.

BE COMFORTABLE IN YOUR LEARNING ENVIRONMENT

Okay, so maybe I was a little too harsh on flex seating before. There is merit to that room arrangement. But as anyone who has ever run flexible seating in a classroom will tell you, you better have your procedural pieces in place or things can quickly get out of hand.

Enter personalized practices.

Similar to many of the personalized practices mentioned before, preparing students for choice in where they sit starts with teacher clarity about the *why*. Explain to students that learning can be enhanced when people are comfortable in their environment. Stress that there is a difference between productively comfortable and passively comfortable. With elementary kiddos, I sometimes reference Goldilocks here: "We don't want to be uncomfortable or too comfortable. Look for a spot that's just right."

Next, begin to walk them through the available seating options. Those may include stand-up desks, beanbag chairs, active-motion stools, energy balls, or even traditional seats with modifications like added bouncy bands, and more. Don't stress over the number or type of choices; we are not in search of the perfect seat. It's about asking learners to be thoughtful about how and where they sit.

Go back to the systematic scaffolding that was outlined in detail in earlier chapters. Talk about the benefits (and behavior expectations) of every style of seat. You might also consider holding a class conversation about behavior norms and consequences when those norms are broken. Then begin to give students a chance to try each choice available, multiple times. Have learners reflect after each learning experience, and eventually, the students will develop a preference.

Inevitably, there is a greater demand for one particular style of seat than there are chairs like that available. Don't worry about that too much. Do your best to be accommodating, which might mean a learner or two gets their second choice. Just continue to add in more pieces when and where you can. However, another way to solve this dilemma is to have students split time between seats, which leads nicely into our next conversation.

GIVE EVERY ACTION A PLACE
TO BE CARRIED OUT

The freedom to choose a seat and stay in it is one choice. The freedom to flexibly switch seats and move around the learning space is another.

Before granting learners the freedom to relocate, you will want to be clear about how and why that might benefit their learning. Sure, there will be times when students move to ask a question, but more often than not, student movement in the space is necessary because the task they are aiming to accomplish has changed and could be better completed elsewhere.

At this point, the advice of educator and learning-space design expert Dr. Robert Dillon comes to mind. Bob's philosophy is that every learning action should have a place to live within the space, and that sentiment has always resonated with me.

From a personalized lens, let's ask, Does the choice being offered need its own space to breathe? If the learning is asynchronous, quite often the answer to this is yes. Therefore, think strategically about how even a room full of traditional desks might be arranged to support learners in the work they're doing.

For example, sometimes the learning follows a linear, step-by-step process. In those instances, if students are permitted to move through those steps asynchronously, designating a station for each step can be helpful.

These linear stations, as we'll call them, can house directions, resources, materials, and more that help learners navigate that specific part of the learning process. This will also seat learners alongside peers who are working on the same step as they are, which is ideal for peer-to-peer support. What's also great is that this layout visually communicates, to the teacher and the students, the general pace of the class through the activity or learning. That awareness can be a major motivator, to all ability levels, in an asynchronous learning environment.

In contrast, there will also be times when the asynchronous learning is nonlinear, as students take different learning pathways or go through a set of assignments in whatever order they choose. When that's the case, stations can still be extremely beneficial; they are just navigated differently.

For example, imagine you are a student who has been given a choice-in-product assignment. You have decided to create a video, while your best friend has committed to drawing a comic book. The materials, devices, and tech tools that each of you needs to create your product will be vastly different, so we will need stations in the space to help with any and all endeavors.

This might mean that there's a writing and revision station, an art-materials station, a tech-tools station, a video and green-screen station, and potentially more. These can simply be spots where student desks are brought together to form groups where materials, support documents, etc. are available for each of these purposes.

In that space, you might begin your video project at the writing station and compose a script for what you intend to say. Next, you could move to the art station and create a prop you need for the video. Then, you would be off to the video station to record, before ending up at the tech station to get help with editing the final project. However, your best friend who is making the comic might only visit one or two of those stations. This nonlinear arrangement offers learners the support and flexibility they need to develop their own path and pace.

Finally, it's useful at times to arrange the desks in the room by the number of students who can meet in each space. In that model, the design acknowledges that different tasks require different group sizes, and so the stations are constructed as a set number of seats, not according to a specific assignment step.

For example, the room might be laid out with two small-group stations at the front where four or more students could meet for one of a number of purposes like receiving direct instruction, collaborating on a project, or taking part in graded (recorded) discussion. Then, the middle of the room might offer desks arranged in pairs—perfect for peer feedback, support with quick questions, partner work, etc. At the back of the room, individual desks might be turned to face the wall, offering learners a chance to learn and work with minimal distractions.

With all three of these approaches, the linear stations, the nonlinear stations, and the group-size model, it's imperative to preface with the same behavior norms and consequences conversation mentioned earlier. Here the personalized practice is more about clearly communicating expectations before you begin and coaching learners to make better choices along the way.

The nuances of that coaching will be addressed in the next section.

TEACH LEARNERS TO SELF-REGULATE AND LIMIT THEIR DISTRACTIONS

Early on in my efforts supporting teachers through this type of thinking, I was sharing about learner choice in the learning space when a teacher raised her hand and said, "You know, this all sounds great. Like, it makes sense and all. But Andrew, you don't know my kids. There's no way they could ever handle this."

Several heads nodded as the room fell quiet, awaiting my response.

"That's exactly the reason why this work is important," I said. "These practices assume that the learners can't do this yet, and they also recognize that reality as being a huge problem. What hope do our students have of being lifelong learners if they can't figure out how to sit down and accomplish something? The work is teaching them to handle this."

I still hold to that belief today. Sure, the process of getting the learners there is nuanced. But it ultimately boils down to asking a student one simple question: What is keeping you from being at your best?

Literally—ask them that question when they are exhibiting off-task behaviors.

When you do, 80-ish percent of the time, you will get an answer that is so honest and on-point that it will shock you. The other 20 percent—the student will play coy or claim to have no idea. Owning your shortcomings can be hard. With the latter situation, instead of reprimanding a learner for off-task behavior, try calmly pointing out that something clearly needs to change because the current approach doesn't seem to be setting them up for success. Don't presume to know what the issues are, even if you have a pretty good idea. Instead, give the learner the choice of self-identifying the behavior or doing so with your support. When presented with this ultimatum, most students will offer an answer. If not, step in and coach them on what behaviors you're seeing that are hindering their ability to learn.

Then it comes down to helping them work through their specific behavior. As I said earlier, it's impossible to speak to every potential need, but below are three of the most frequent issues along with a brief insight on what to suggest the learner do to regain their focus.

- **IF THE NOISE IN THE LEARNING SPACE IS DISTRACTING,** recommend that learners use headphones when working independently. Point out that listening to their favorite songs, searching for songs on YouTube, or shuffling through the music library on their device can actually do more harm than good. Research has shown that lyric-less music is recommended for concentration, so start there. While writing this book, Tara Martin taught me about the benefits of alpha waves on productivity, which was a game changer for me, personally. To help you help your students focus, I've created and shared several links to Spotify and YouTube productivity playlists on my website, AndrewDEaston.com. This strategy can dramatically improve learner productivity.

- **IF THE MOVEMENT IN THE LEARNING SPACE IS DISTRACTING,** tell students they have the option of repositioning their desks to face the wall.

- **IF A GROUP OF FRIENDS IS BEING CHATTY,** the traditional approach to solving this issue would be to assign them seats in different corners of the room. Instead, give them a chance or two to correct the behavior, with the understanding that otherwise the group will be broken up. If it comes to that, the students then get to pick where they sit next, so long as they are no longer seated next to those same friends. I once saw a learner move four times before he found the place in the room that helped him be productive. Years later, he came back to tell me that he still asks his teachers if he can reposition his desk in that way because he came to realize that it helps him that much.

CHAPTER 12

LAYERING MULTIPLE LEARNER-CHOICE OPPORTUNITIES INTO THE LEARNING

From the very first sentence in this chapter, I want to stress that the decision to implement any choice opportunities should be made according to things like the level of responsibility the learners can handle, the teacher's ability to provide effective scaffolding and support, and the amount of flexibility for choice that the curriculum affords. In short, it's better to do one thing well than get competitive and force-fit choices when the learners aren't ready for them.

However, if you think of each choice as its own chunk of responsibility, having more choices equates to the learner having a greater degree of ownership over the learning process. That's why stacking these opportunities is the path to true learner-centered and learner-driven learning.

Once you feel confident with offering one choice, look for an opportunity to add a second that enhances the first. For example, intentional learning-space design makes an excellent complement to almost any choice. Or, if your learners have the ability to make their own choice-in-instruction decisions, a logical next step might be to lead them through some choice-in-processing-strategy practices. It's okay to ask students to continue to demonstrate their autonomy in one choice area, while also teaching them how to grow in another.

Through time and practice, I was able to grow to a point where virtually all of the choices outlined in this book were offered within the same learning experience. Here's what that looked like:

The unit of study was a science fiction unit at the high school level, where students had control over the pace of their learning for a five-week period of time. Two days before the unit began, the learners took a pretest, created their own unit calendar, and began researching the novel options available to them in this choice unit.

The class period before the unit began, learners picked up their books, received their pretest results, and scheduled themselves to attend the live lectures that would address any specific needs indicated by the pretest data. Next, students were given a short window of time to informally plan when and with whom they would meet to hold their two required graded discussions. Some students scheduled future class periods, others chose to meet after school, and some elected to record their conversations while at home using Zoom or Google Meet. With the time that was left, we discussed the summative assignments and their respective prompts.

On the first day of the unit, students entered the classroom and, having previously learned about learning-space design, moved the desks out of rows and into the areas that they needed according to the group dynamics necessary for the various assignments. Once seated, they took out their daily goals form, referenced their calendar, and set a SMART goal to complete by the end of class that day.

Prior to the start of class, I walked around the room welcoming the learners, checking daily goals, and reminding certain individuals that their pretest scores had made it mandatory for them to attend the live lecture (which needed to be reflected in their daily goals).

By the time the bell sounded for class to begin, everyone had already begun learning. For the first five minutes of actual class time, I finished checking daily goals, touching base with anyone who may have been absent, and answering any written questions the learners had recorded on their daily goals handout.

Then I announced that the day's live lecture was about to begin.

Roughly a third of the class stood up and moved to the front to attend the ten-to-fifteen-minute microlearning opportunity. During that live lecture, learners used their preferred processing strategies while I taught. At the same time, the other two-thirds of the class were either reading (using their choice annotation strategy) or navigating the LMS to access the assignments, their instructions, and any materials they needed, like video resources, digital handouts, and more. Most of these documents were also available as hard-copy handouts. Some learners worked independently, others sat with a partner, some sat on the floor, and later in the unit, a small group might gather to record a graded discussion.

Around the twenty-minute mark, the live lecture ended and the learners returned to their seats. I then took a lap around the room to see if any new questions had come up during that fifteen-minute window of time. If there were no questions, I would either sit in on a graded discussion, give feedback on a choice-in-product effort, or walk around the room casually asking learners, "How's it going?" I would stay active and available while also using proximity as a classroom management tool.

With five minutes left in class, students were prompted to reflect on their learning for the day and assign themselves homework or adjust their calendars as needed.

This rhythm continued for the duration of that five-week window of time. The first four weeks were for formative work, and while learners could submit work early, all the formatives had a hard deadline of the end of the fourth week.

This left one week at the end of the unit for summative work. Learners were asked to complete a series of written assessments and also to create a product to demonstrate their learning. Since the prompts and expectations had been communicated before the unit began, learners knew that if they finished their formative work early, they could allocate more class time to the choice-in-product summative.

I share this story here because previously we discussed each choice in isolation. And while I stand by the belief that every choice opportunity holds great value toward informing learners how to better personalize their experience, when the choices are layered, it asks for something more. Employing multiple personalized strategies, with little to no prompting, across the various facets of the learning process and all within the same class period (and across multiple weeks' worth of learning) is without question the best example of learner-driven personalization that I have ever seen, heard, or read about. And it was done in a public school with a traditional grading scale and bell schedule, with district-issued curriculum, on a team where every section of the course had a common start and end date, and with common formatives and summatives.

CHAPTER 13

BRAINSTORMING FOR ENTRY POINTS

In my time supporting teachers with this work, I have found that the majority of educators seem to begin either by identifying a specific place to start, like a lesson or unit, or by earmarking a specific choice as the option that they are most comfortable offering next.

If the latter makes the most sense to you, then the process is fairly straightforward. Ask yourself where in your current curriculum might it make sense to offer learners that specific choice, then build in personalized practices moving backward from there.

However, if your preferred approach is to select an upcoming lesson or unit and build in the choices from there, the process will look a little different. The first question that comes up is how will you know which unit to select. If you're having trouble deciding, here are a few common justifications for why educators opt to add choices, personalized practices, or both to a lesson or unit. Teachers often choose:

- Lessons or units that are traditionally weak in learner engagement. In this case, empowering the learner to drive the learning can add new energy to the experience.

- Lessons or units where choice already exists, and they then build in personalized practices that truly prepare learners to own that chance to make a decision.
- Lessons or units where differentiation already exists. Such experiences typically have a wealth of resources that can be utilized for creating choice-in-pace experiences.
- Lessons or units that are new to the course or the teacher. If you are going to be building something from scratch, why not build it with learner choice?
- Lessons or units with assignments that follow a linear progression and/or have a lot of work time. Give students the flexibility to work at their own pace whenever possible.
- Lessons or units that follow the state test. Many teachers opt to try new things once the high stakes of a statewide assessment are over, so consider beginning this work in that window of time.

Having selected where in your curriculum to offer learners some degree of choice, the next step will be to determine which choice(s) you will make available. Independently or as a team, take a moment to work through this graphic organizer. It will help you entertain what choices might be available across this learning experience. Use the bottom row to help you think through what personalized practices you could implement as scaffolding to ensure that the learners are prepared to handle the responsibility that comes with each choice.

	The Choice(s) Is this choice possible, Yes or No. If Yes, take brainstorming notes on where and how that choice could be made available.	The Personalized Practice(s) For every Yes, create brainstorming notes on how you will teach the students to make academically sound decisions when that choice is finally made available to them.
Learner Choice in Topic		
Learner Choice in Instruction		
Learner Choice in Strategy		
Learner Choice in Product		
Learner Choice in Pace		
Learner Choice in Communication		
Learner Choice in Learning Space		

Please note that just because you recognize that the lesson or unit you selected has the potential for multiple choice opportunities, it does not mean you have to do all of them the first time out. It's okay (and quite frankly, I would encourage you) to pick one or even two choices to begin with and save any others for future iterations of that lesson or unit (or ones similar to it).

CHAPTER 14

MEASURING THE IMPACT OF THIS WORK

In education, how we measure student learning and educator effectiveness is always somewhat of a slippery thing. There's the obvious argument that test scores are the most accurate predictor, but as any good educator will tell you, there is so much more to teaching and learning than that.

I've always agreed with William Bruce Cameron's idea that "not everything that can be counted counts and not everything that counts can be counted."[1] I think about this a lot when conversations about data-driven teaching and learning arise. Here's all I know. Setting goals is a meaningful thing in all aspects of life. Being able to measure progress toward those goals is an essential step in achieving them. However, the decision-making and commitment that goes into determining what gets measured and how it gets measured should be largely under the control of the people those goals seek to serve. In this case, that means the teachers and ultimately the students.

Ownership is critical for meaningful change, and so once again, it's a matter of choice. If fostering learner agency and creating a more

---

1 William Bruce Cameron, *Informal Sociology: A Casual Introduction to Sociological Thinking* (New York: Random House, 1963).

equitable learning experience for all students is of value to you as an individual or institution, this chapter will offer choice-in-evaluation options that can help you measure the impact that your efforts are having on the learning taking place.

EVALUATE PERSONALIZATION USING AN INSTRUCTIONAL FRAMEWORK

For the sake of brevity here, we will look at two of the more prominent instructional frameworks in education today, those of Danielson and Marzano.

The first three domains of Danielson's Framework for Teaching focus on planning and preparation, the classroom environment, and instruction. Using the language that already exists in the Danielson evaluation tool, any of the single-choice personalized practices would score well in this framework. When multiple learner-choice opportunities are layered in together, there's not a component within those first three domains that is not addressed.

The most important point to make here is that within those components, educators are encouraged to evolve in their practices from a rating of *3-Proficient* to a *4-Distinguished*, and generally speaking, that occurs when the learner's role is shifted to the center of the learning process. In short, personalized practices help educators empower their learners to drive their own learning, which in turn leads to a substantive improvement according to the Danielson evaluation tool.

It's no surprise then that the Marzano Instructional Framework measures follow a similar narrative. The first two domains in Marzano's framework, "Classroom Strategies and Behaviors" and "Planning and Preparation," consist of forty-nine design elements. Forty of those forty-nine have been addressed by the personalized practices outlined in this book, with the majority of those nine omissions falling under situational experiences like playing academic games or reviewing.

What the personalized practices deeply address is the planning-for-diverse-learners piece in Marzano's work, which can be a real challenge to design for when the teacher is the one who is expected to do this *for* the learner.

EVALUATE PERSONALIZATION USING HATTIE'S VISIBLE LEARNING EFFECT-SIZE LIST

John Hattie's efforts with *Visible Learning* led him to develop a list of over 250 factors that influence learning, and his research produced an effect size for each factor that essentially quantifies its impact on student learning (positively or negatively).

Hattie's model affords us an opportunity to assess personalized practices by comparing the previous practices to the pedagogical improvements being made through personalization.

For example, let's say that a teacher has taught Unit X in a traditional and consistent manner for the past five years, and now their plan is to add some personalization to it. They implement personalized practices as scaffolding prior to the launch of the unit, and then during Unit X, students own the pace, the instructional delivery modality, and how they show what they know on the end-of-unit, summative product.

At the end of Unit X, the teacher can reflect on the enhancements provided by the choice opportunities and, using Hattie's list, tally up the effect-size difference that those collective improvements had on impacting learning.

KEEP IT SWEET AND SIMPLE

Okay, if we want to operate under the assumption that there is an inherent value in teaching students strategies for how to be better at learning and that more learner choice leads to greater levels of academic ownership and agency, then the most straightforward form of data and record keeping would note how often learners have these experiences.

Teachers appreciate the simplicity of these personalized practices because the goal is clear: create more opportunities for learner choice. That is both communicable and measurable when it comes to setting professional goals. If last semester you focused on implementing one choice and learning to do that well, then this semester the goal becomes a second, and so on.

When I work in support of schools, we often develop an evaluative rubric that marks educator progress with personalization simply by how many personalized practices are implemented along with a choice experience for learners to drive. If you are interested in such a measure, you can learn more about it at AndrewDEaston.com.

Ultimately, good educators know what good teaching looks like. It's something that can be felt in the room. It's there in the moment when the proverbial light comes on for a student, and wow, does the afterglow from that light carry on to impact their teacher, their peers, and their future learning thereafter. Teachers know what true focus looks like, and that academic confidence has both a presence and an energy when it lives within a child. Ownership of learning is powerful, visible, and real, and personalized practices enhance each learner's capacity to do just that—confidently drive their own experience.

CHAPTER 15

CONCLUSION

When I began this journey with personalizing learning, I did so because I had a heart for my students and knew we needed to enhance their access to the learning and their ability to be effective learners for the rest of their lives. This added a layer of purpose to what we were doing in class, which in turn added additional depth to the relationships I had with each of them.

As time has gone on and I have had opportunities to share about personalized practices with others, I still see my former students' faces in my mind as I recall specific conversations that led to the next practice, the next revision, the next step forward with personalizing learning. No doubt the work of an educator is always personal, but what I've come to realize is that by first teaching and then trusting students to lead, they feel recognized and responsible in a way that brings meaning and confidence to all they do.

And what is best for learners is also best for educators.

It has been deeply rewarding to support educators as they learn how to design personalized learning experiences for their students because this work practices what it preaches. This approach to personalization honors that teaching is an art and that practitioners have a right to expect that they too will be empowered to choose with things like where to begin, where to grow next, and how to turn the why behind this work into an opportunity to move their learners closer to their learning potential.

ACKNOWLEDGMENTS

Writing a book is much harder than I thought and more rewarding than I could have ever imagined. None of this would have been possible without the love, support, and learning I have been blessed to experience over the course of my career.

To my colleagues at Gardner-Edgerton High School, thank you all for welcoming me into this profession and giving me the space to grow as a practitioner. I love and appreciate you all more than you know.

To my colleagues at Westside High School and across District 66, thank you for the opportunities you gave me to learn, serve, and lead alongside you. Thank you, Mark Weichel, for your mentorship, guidance, and friendship.

To my family and friends who were there for me through the writing and revision process, I am truly grateful for the time, space, and emotional support you have always provided.

Thank you, Dave and Shelley Burgess, for the chance to share this work with the world, and many thanks to Tara Martin, who has always inspired me and supported my pursuit of this goal.

Finally, Amour and Andrew, I want you to know that every time I speak, write, or hit Record, my hope is to be the kind of passionate educator I would want for each of you. You both mean so very much to me and are my inspiration.

ABOUT
ANDREW EASTON

Andrew Easton is an author, speaker, podcaster, consultant, and all-around advocate for education. He is a high-energy presenter who loves learning and collaborating with others.

Andrew is an award-winning teacher whose work with developing and implementing innovative practices in his classroom makes him an authentic voice on a variety of topics. He is a leader in the areas of personalized learning, blended learning, games in education, instructional video production, remote teaching and learning, learning-space design, ed leadership, and social-emotional learning. For over fifteen years, Andrew has passionately supported hundreds of educators, and he has experience leading schools and districts in their efforts to scale up the personalization of learning. His message focuses on fostering both the mindset and the methodology needed to successfully integrate personalized practices into a school culture while also recognizing that each teacher brings their own sensibility and style to how they lead learning in their classroom.

For a comprehensive look at the breadth of his work and speaking topics, access Andrew's website at AndrewDEaston.com, where you can also connect with him via his social media.

BIBLIOGRAPHY

Basye, Dale. "Personalized vs. Differentiated vs. Individualized Learning." ISTE blog. January 24, 2018. iste.org/explore/ Education-leadership/Personalized-vs.-differentiated- vs.-individualized-learning.

Bray, Barbara, and Kathleen McClaskey. *How to Personalize Learning: A Practical Guide for Getting Started and Going Deeper.* Thousand Oaks, CA: Corwin, 2017.

Cameron, William Bruce. *Informal Sociology: A Casual Introduction to Sociological Thinking.* New York: Random House, 1963.

Collins, Jim. *Good to Great: Why Some Companies Make the Leap ... and Others Don't.* New York: Collins, 2009.

Danielson, Charlotte. *The Framework for Teaching Evaluation Instrument, 2013 Edition: The Newest Rubric Enhancing the Links to the Common Dore State Standards.* Princeton, NJ: Danielson Group, 2013.

Dillon, Robert. Conversation with the author. March 16, 2018.

Froelich, Mandy. Conversation with the author. June 2019.

Hall, Pete, and Alisa A. Simeral. *Creating a Culture of Reflective Practice: Capacity Building for Schoolwide Success.* Alexandria, VA: ASCD, 2017.

Hattie, John. "Hattie Ranking: 252 Influences and Effect Sizes Related to Student Achievement." Visible Learning blog. 2018. visible-learning.org/hattie-ranking-influences-effect -sizes-learning-achievement/.

Kallack, Bena, and Allison Zmuda. *Students at the Center: Personalized Learning with Habits of Mind.* Alexandria, VA: ASCD, 2017.

Lubbock, John. *The Beauties of Nature and the Wonders of the World We Live in.* New York: Macmillan, 1892.

Martin, Tara. "#BookSnaps." Be REAL blog. August 23, 2016. tarammartin.com/booksnaps-snapping-for-learning/.

Marzano, Robert J. *The Handbook for the New Art and Science of Teaching: Your Guide to the Marzano Framework for Competency-Based Education and Teaching Methods.* Bloomington, IN: Solution Tree Press, 2018.

Nadella, Satya. Quoted in "The Next Great Disruption Is Hybrid Work—Are We Ready?." Microsoft. March 22, 2021. microsoft.com/en-us/worklab/work-trend-index/ hybrid-work.

Ozimek, Adam. "Future Workforce Report 2021: How Remote Work Is Changing Business Forever." Upwork. September 28, 2021. upwork.com/research/future-workforce-report.

Parrish, Sherry. *Number Talks: Whole Number Computation.* Sausalito, CA: Math Solutions, 2014).

Rickabaugh, James. *Tapping the Power of Personalized Learning: A Roadmap for School Leaders.* Alexandria, VA: ASCD, 2016.

Sparks, Sarah D. "Differentiated Instruction: A Primer." Education Week. January 28, 2015. edweek.org/teaching-learning/ differentiated-instruction-a-primer/2015/01.

Sturgis, Chris. "Policies for Personalization: Student Agency." Aurora Institute blog. November 1, 2016. aurora-institute.org/cw_post/ policies-for-personalization-student-agency/.

MORE FROM

Since 2012, DBCI has published books that inspire and equip educators to be their best. For more information on our titles or to purchase bulk orders for your school, district, or book study, visit DaveBurgessConsulting.com/DBCIbooks.

Like a PIRATE™ Series
Teach Like a PIRATE by Dave Burgess
eXPlore Like a PIRATE by Michael Matera
Learn Like a PIRATE by Paul Solarz
Plan Like a PIRATE by Dawn M. Harris
Play Like a PIRATE by Quinn Rollins
Run Like a PIRATE by Adam Welcome
Tech Like a PIRATE by Matt Miller

Lead Like a PIRATE™ Series
Lead Like a PIRATE by Shelley Burgess and Beth Houf
Balance Like a PIRATE by Jessica Cabeen, Jessica Johnson, and
    Sarah Johnson
Lead beyond Your Title by Nili Bartley
Lead with Appreciation by Amber Teamann and Melinda Miller
Lead with Culture by Jay Billy
Lead with Instructional Rounds by Vicki Wilson
Lead with Literacy by Mandy Ellis
She Leads by Dr. Rachael George and Majalise W. Tolan

Leadership & School Culture

Beyond the Surface of Restorative Practices by Marisol Rerucha

Change the Narrative by Henry J. Turner and Kathy Lopes

Choosing to See by Pamela Seda and Kyndall Brown

Culturize by Jimmy Casas

Discipline Win by Andy Jacks

Escaping the School Leader's Dunk Tank by Rebecca Coda and
     Rick Jetter

Fight Song by Kim Bearden

From Teacher to Leader by Starr Sackstein

If the Dance Floor Is Empty, Change the Song by Joe Clark

The Innovator's Mindset by George Couros

It's OK to Say "They" by Christy Whittlesey

Kids Deserve It! by Todd Nesloney and Adam Welcome

Let Them Speak by Rebecca Coda and Rick Jetter

The Limitless School by Abe Hege and Adam Dovico

Live Your Excellence by Jimmy Casas

Next-Level Teaching by Jonathan Alsheimer

The Pepper Effect by Sean Gaillard

Principaled by Kate Barker, Kourtney Ferrua, and Rachael George

The Principled Principal by Jeffrey Zoul and Anthony McConnell

Relentless by Hamish Brewer

The Secret Solution by Todd Whitaker, Sam Miller, and Ryan Donlan

Start. Right. Now. by Todd Whitaker, Jeffrey Zoul, and Jimmy Casas

Stop. Right. Now. by Jimmy Casas and Jeffrey Zoul

Teachers Deserve It by Rae Hughart and Adam Welcome

Teach Your Class Off by CJ Reynolds

They Call Me "Mr. De" by Frank DeAngelis

Thrive through the Five by Jill M. Siler

Unmapped Potential by Julie Hasson and Missy Lennard

When Kids Lead by Todd Nesloney and Adam Dovico

Word Shift by Joy Kirr

Your School Rocks by Ryan McLane and Eric Lowe

Technology & Tools

50 Things to Go Further with Google Classroom by Alice Keeler and
Libbi Miller

50 Things You Can Do with Google Classroom by Alice Keeler and
Libbi Miller

140 Twitter Tips for Educators by Brad Currie, Billy Krakower, and
Scott Rocco

Block Breaker by Brian Aspinall

Building Blocks for Tiny Techies by Jamila "Mia" Leonard

Code Breaker by Brian Aspinall

The Complete EdTech Coach by Katherine Goyette and Adam Juarez

Control Alt Achieve by Eric Curts

The Esports Education Playbook by Chris Aviles, Steve Isaacs,
Christine Lion-Bailey, and Jesse Lubinsky

Google Apps for Littles by Christine Pinto and Alice Keeler

Master the Media by Julie Smith

Raising Digital Leaders by Jennifer Casa-Todd

Reality Bytes by Christine Lion-Bailey, Jesse Lubinsky, and Micah
Shippee, PhD

Sail the 7 Cs with Microsoft Education by Becky Keene and
Kathi Kersznowski

Shake Up Learning by Kasey Bell

Social LEADia by Jennifer Casa-Todd

Stepping Up to Google Classroom by Alice Keeler and
Kimberly Mattina

Teaching Math with Google Apps by Alice Keeler and
Diana Herrington

Teachingland by Amanda Fox and Mary Ellen Weeks

Teaching with Google Jamboard by Alice Keeler and
Kimberly Mattina

Teaching Methods & Materials

All 4s and 5s by Andrew Sharos

Boredom Busters by Katie Powell

The Classroom Chef by John Stevens and Matt Vaudrey

The Collaborative Classroom by Trevor Muir

Copyrighteous by Diana Gill

CREATE by Bethany J. Petty

Deploying EduProtocols by Kim Voge, with Jon Corippo and
    Marlena Hebern

Ditch That Homework by Matt Miller and Alice Keeler

Ditch That Textbook by Matt Miller

Don't Ditch That Tech by Matt Miller, Nate Ridgway, and
    Angelia Ridgway

EDrenaline Rush by John Meehan

Educated by Design by Michael Cohen, The Tech Rabbi

The EduProtocol Field Guide by Marlena Hebern and Jon Corippo

The EduProtocol Field Guide: Book 2 by Marlena Hebern and
    Jon Corippo

The EduProtocol Field Guide: Math Edition by Lisa Nowakowski and
    Jeremiah Ruesch

The EduProtocol Field Guide: Social Studies Edition by Dr. Scott M.
    Petri and Adam Moler

Expedition Science by Becky Schnekser

Frustration Busters by Katie Powell

Fully Engaged by Michael Matera and John Meehan

Game On? Brain On! by Lindsay Portnoy, PhD

Guided Math AMPED by Reagan Tunstall

Innovating Play by Jessica LaBar-Twomy and Christine Pinto

Instructional Coaching Connection by Nathan Lang-Raad

Instant Relevance by Denis Sheeran

Keeping the Wonder by Jenna Copper, Ashley Bible, Abby Gross, and
    Staci Lamb

LAUNCH by John Spencer and A.J. Juliani

Learning in the Zone by Dr. Sonny Magana
Lights, Cameras, TEACH! by Kevin J. Butler
Make Learning MAGICAL by Tisha Richmond
Pass the Baton by Kathryn Finch and Theresa Hoover
Project-Based Learning Anywhere by Lori Elliott
Pure Genius by Don Wettrick
The Revolution by Darren Ellwein and Derek McCoy
Shift This! by Joy Kirr
Skyrocket Your Teacher Coaching by Michael Cary Sonbert
Spark Learning by Ramsey Musallam
Sparks in the Dark by Travis Crowder and Todd Nesloney
Table Talk Math by John Stevens
Unpack Your Impact by Naomi O'Brien and LaNesha Tabb
The Wild Card by Hope and Wade King
Writefully Empowered by Jacob Chastain
The Writing on the Classroom Wall by Steve Wyborney
You Are Poetry by Mike Johnston

Inspiration, Professional Growth & Personal Development

Be REAL by Tara Martin
Be the One for Kids by Ryan Sheehy
The Coach ADVenture by Amy Illingworth
Creatively Productive by Lisa Johnson
Educational Eye Exam by Alicia Ray
The EduNinja Mindset by Jennifer Burdis
Empower Our Girls by Lynmara Colón and Adam Welcome
Finding Lifelines by Andrew Grieve and Andrew Sharos
The Four O'Clock Faculty by Rich Czyz
How Much Water Do We Have? by Pete and Kris Nunweiler
P Is for Pirate by Dave and Shelley Burgess
A Passion for Kindness by Tamara Letter
The Path to Serendipity by Allyson Apsey

Rogue Leader by Rich Czyz

Sanctuaries by Dan Tricarico

Saving Sycamore by Molly B. Hudgens

The SECRET SAUCE by Rich Czyz

Shattering the Perfect Teacher Myth by Aaron Hogan

Stories from Webb by Todd Nesloney

Talk to Me by Kim Bearden

Teach Better by Chad Ostrowski, Tiffany Ott, Rae Hughart, and
    Jeff Gargas

Teach Me, Teacher by Jacob Chastain

Teach, Play, Learn! by Adam Peterson

The Teachers of Oz by Herbie Raad and Nathan Lang-Raad

TeamMakers by Laura Robb and Evan Robb

Through the Lens of Serendipity by Allyson Apsey

The Zen Teacher by Dan Tricarico

Children's Books

Alpert by LaNesha Tabb

Alpert & Friends by LaNesha Tabb

Beyond Us by Aaron Polansky

Cannonball In by Tara Martin

Dolphins in Trees by Aaron Polansky

I Can Achieve Anything by MoNique Waters

I Want to Be a Lot by Ashley Savage

Micah's Big Question by Naomi O'Brien

The Princes of Serendip by Allyson Apsey

Ride with Emilio by Richard Nares

A Teacher's Top Secret Confidential by LaNesha Tabb

A Teacher's Top Secret: Mission Accomplished by LaNesha Tabb

The Wild Card Kids by Hope and Wade King

Zom-Be a Design Thinker by Amanda Fox

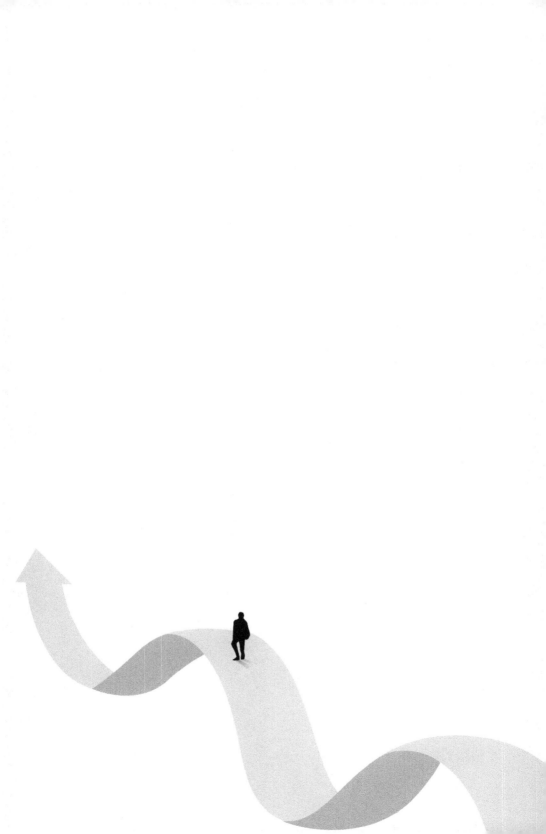

Made in the USA
Monee, IL
10 February 2023